WICKED GOOD
BARBECUE

FEARLESS RECIPES FROM TWO DAMN YANKEES
WHO WON THE BIGGEST, BADDEST
BBQ COMPETITIONS IN THE WORLD

ANDY HUSBANDS and CHRIS HART
with ANDREA PYENSON
★ PHOTOGRAPHY BY KEN GOODMAN ★

FAIR WINDS
PRESS
BEVERLY, MASSACHUSETTS

This edition published in the USA in 2015 by
Fair Winds Press, a member of
Quarto Publishing Group USA Inc.
100 Cummings Center
Suite 406-L
Beverly, MA 01915-6101
www.fairwindspress.com
Visit www.QuarrySPOON.com and help us celebrate food and culture one spoonful at a time!

19 18 17 16 15   1 2 3 4 5

ISBN: 978-1-59233-684-5

Digital edition published in 2012
eISBN: 978-1-61058-210-0

Library of Congress Cataloging-in-Publication Data available

Book design by Carol Holtz
Book layout by meganjonesdesign.com
Photography by Ken Goodman Photography
Additional photography by Caitlin Bilodeau, Frank Boyer, Todd Coleman, Jessica Goodman, and Jenny Hart

Printed and bound in China

FOR OUR FAMILIES.

★ CONTENTS ★

CHAPTER 4

TWISTED TRADITIONALS 90

CHAPTER 5

D.I.Y. BBQ (FRANKENCUE) 134

FOREWORD

I first met Andy Husbands at the East Coast Grill, the celebrated restaurant in Cambridge, Massachusetts, that launched the revolution in contemporary American grilling.

We reconnected last year at a barbecue I staged for the crew of the USS *Constitution* ("Old Ironsides," the world's oldest commissioned warship afloat), where Andy did a terrific job preparing a meal from my book, *Planet Barbecue* (Workman, 2010)—a feat that was equally remarkable for the fidelity with which he executed my recipes and the skill with which he turned them out on his custom-built smoker.

After that experience, I vowed that the next time I met Andy it would be over his food. I was particularly interested in some of the dishes he and his co-author and IQUE barbecue teammate, Chris Hart, made to win some of the biggest, toughest barbecue competitions in the world. Like the Jack Daniel's World Championship Invitational Barbecue in Lynchburg, Tennessee, where IQUE took the Grand Championship with their astonishingly succulent, smoky spare ribs. (You can read all about them on page 29.) Or the American Royal in Kansas City, where IQUE's beef marinade-injected brisket beat out hundreds of competitors to be named the competition's top slab of beef (see page 43). Not bad for any smoke-meisters. Downright astonishing for a bunch of Yankees!

Well, now I have something even better—the secrets to their success—in the form of a breathtakingly original, meticulously detailed, lavishly illustrated cookbook that's as piquant and sassy as the food IQUE serves to smoke the competition. It gives me great pleasure to introduce *Wicked Good Barbecue*.

These guys are a rarity—chefs who not only talk the talk, but also walk the walk, turning out dishes like the Seven-Layer Dip of Disbelief (an IQUE riff on the traditional bean dip that includes layers of Old Bay–seasoned shredded beef short ribs and crab remoulade), Six-Day Bacon of the Gods, Whole Smoke-Roasted Striped Bass, the Ultimate Steak Bomb, Pot Likker and Cornmeal Dumplings, and Pecan Pie–Stuffed Cheesecake for dessert. Did I mention the Motel 6 Old-Fashioned, which comes complete with advice on making simple syrup in your motel room?

They go beyond straight competition barbecue food to ambitious—some might say outrageous—recipes that are worth every minute of preparation that goes into them. With detailed instructions for each dish, as well as explanations of different barbecue styles, techniques, equipment, and more, Husbands and Hart urge readers to "get outside and start smoking!"

I can only add: Amen.

—STEVEN RAICHLEN,
AUTHOR OF *PLANET BARBECUE* AND HOST
OF *PRIMAL GRILL* ON PBS, 2011

INTRODUCTION

How did two guys from Boston win hundreds of barbecue ribbons, thirty Kansas City Barbeque Society championships, and the biggest prize of them all, the Jack Daniel's World Championship Invitational Barbecue? It took about twelve years, lots of hard work, a healthy sense of youthful invincibility seasoned with a dash of arrogance, more fun than we might even be able to remember, and the help of our IQUE barbecue teammates. And now we're ready to share the secrets that got us here—well, most of them anyway. Some things that happened in Kansas City will have to stay in Kansas City.

When we started, we were part of a relatively small but devout bunch of folks who loved nothing more than spending a few days at a time hanging with friends, drinking bourbon and beer, playing late-night poker, cooking over live fire—and trying to prove that we did all of it better than everybody else around us.

A lot has changed in ten years. We still love doing all those things. And when we compete, we're in it to win. But that devout bunch is not so small any more. In this new century, barbecue competitions have become one of the fastest growing "sports" in the United States. The American Royal in Kansas City routinely draws more than 500 teams to compete. And barbecue organizations are multiplying throughout the country. We see this not only as a reflection of how many people appreciate great barbecue, but also how many people appreciate great food. And the lengths they're going to these days to experience it.

In the world of food television, blogs, chat rooms, and publications, where it's not uncommon for people to photograph their every meal, then beam the shots over the Internet, these same folks are taking the time to seek out the best ingredients they can find, whether it's American Wagyu from Idaho or heirloom chile peppers from New Mexico. This same food revolution has spilled over into the world of barbecue and live-fire cooking. Inspired barbecue enthusiasts travel miles for that perfect rib/pulled pork sandwich/barbecued bologna they read about on an online forum. They trade recipes and tips online. And they spend hours, sometimes days, making the ultimate dish. Then making it again, and again, and again . . . until they get it right.

Some might call this extreme cooking. We call it what we do. What we've always done. And our reward is that buzz you get when you push yourself to the edge. Sometimes that means standing in the middle of a NASCAR racetrack in Dover, Delaware, at midnight with a tornado barreling down, watching it blow by as you tend to your brisket and pork butts. Sometimes it means waking up every hour through a Saturday night to make sure your fire doesn't go out because you're having company the next day—or because you're just testing recipes. Always it leads to food that's not just really, really tasty, but wicked good.

That's the level of food we have pulled together in this barbecue book. We don't want to scare anybody off, but most of these recipes are not the kind that can be whipped up an hour or so before they are to be served. We often get asked to write recipes like that, usually during football season when the editor of a local newspaper asks us for barbecue tailgate recipes and adds, "Keep it simple." For our book, we thought, "Let's take a different approach. Let's assume our readers' top priority isn't that the food be easy to prepare. Let's assume they want to be challenged, to do whatever it takes to make championship-level barbecue, even if they aren't necessarily planning to compete."

This book is for those people, for you—the barbecue enthusiasts, food geeks, tailgaters, and anybody else who wants to impress the hell out of their family and friends and is willing to put in a little effort to do it. You might need special equipment; you might have to search for some ingredients you don't encounter every day, like oxtail, ghost chiles, or meat glue (don't worry, we'll help you find them). You'll have to spend eight hours to make the best ribs you will ever experience, go through 25 steps to get to barbecue chicken, and make your own sauces and rubs. But trust us, it's worth it.

We entered our first barbecue competition in 1998, almost as a lark. Our performance reflected our lack of preparation. We've come a long way since then, and we have the trophies to prove it. More important, we have the experiences and the knowledge to share. If you want to become a World Barbecue Champion, this book will help you get there (unless you're competing against us), with our exact barbecue competition recipes and many other live-fire creations. If you just want to make some Wicked Good Barbecue, and enjoy it with people you love, we have that covered, too.

IQUE AWARDS

2011 STATE CHAMPIONS—NEW YORK

2010 TEAM OF THE YEAR—NEW ENGLAND BARBECUE SOCIETY

2010 TEAM OF THE YEAR—EMPIRE STATE BARBECUE CHAMPIONSHIP, NEW YORK

2009 GRAND CHAMPIONS—JACK DANIEL'S WORLD CHAMPIONSHIP INVITATIONAL BARBECUE

2006 AND 2008 COOK'S CHOICE CHAMPIONS—JACK DANIEL'S WORLD CHAMPIONSHIP
    INVITATIONAL BARBECUE

2007 1ST PLACE BRISKET—AMERICAN ROYAL BARBECUE COMPETITION

FOUR-TIME TEAM OF THE YEAR—NEW ENGLAND BARBECUE SOCIETY

TEN-TIME INVITEE—JACK DANIEL'S WORLD CHAMPIONSHIP
    INVITATIONAL BARBECUE

MORE THAN THIRTY KANSAS CITY BARBEQUE SOCIETY GRAND CHAMPIONSHIP TITLES

CHAPTER 1

THE BASICS OF BARBECUE

BARBECUE IS VERY SIMILAR to making wine or brewing beer—a craft in which both the science and the art need to be embraced. There are a number of factors that affect a given dish, such as the fat content of the pork, the thickness of a rack of ribs, the humidity inside your smoker, and the elevation at which you cook, so no matter how explicit a recipe is, you will also have to learn to rely on your senses to tell when a dish is perfectly done. After you've been doing it for a while, you'll know by sight when coals are hot enough to start cooking, by touch when a steak is ready, by smell when you left that fish in the smoker too long. Although we have written extremely detailed recipes based on our years of experience, you will increasingly trust your instincts, too.

As with anything you learn to do well, the first step toward barbecue greatness is mastering the basics. On the competition trail, we continually see new teams, with very little experience, show up and try all sorts of tricks they learned about how to win barbecue contests. At the end of the weekend, they're consistently mystified when they end up in the bottom third of the standings.

As a successful team, we are often asked for advice by these newbies. And we often respond with a question: Can you create an excellent piece of barbecue with nothing more than a slab of meat, some dry rub, and fire? They don't usually like that response, and we do go on to give them some more concrete advice. Which is what we're about to give you. (But by the way, for barbecue greatness, the answer to that first question has to be a resounding YES!)

STYLES OF BARBECUE

Discussions of barbecue can get pretty heated, with passions running high over what constitutes "true" barbecue. In the eastern parts of North Carolina, for example, barbecue is whole hog with vinegar-based sauce; head to the western parts of the state, though, and it's pork shoulder with a bit of tomato added to the sauce. Texas is all about beef, salt, pepper, post oak, and not much else; sauce is discouraged. Kansas City features one of our favorites: burnt ends. In Kentucky, the local specialty is slow-cooked mutton served with vinegar dip. In Memphis, you will be eating pork ribs, either slathered in sweet barbecue sauce or "dry," with only a spice rub for seasoning.

We're pretty easy. As far as we're concerned, if it's meat, and it's cooked over fire and smoke at low heat, it's barbecue. However, we respect the regional approaches to barbecue and greatly enjoy cooking in the style of a particular region of the country. The key to cooking great barbecue, though, is not the chosen flavor profile or whether or not to use barbecue sauce. The key is being in full control of your smoker and being able to maintain rock-steady temperatures over long periods of time.

COOKING WITH FIRE

The two main techniques that we use for the majority of the recipes in this book are barbecue (smoking) and grill roasting. The others are described in detail in the individual recipes.

Barbecue: smoking food at 225 to 275°F (110 to 140°C), using indirect heat and charcoal/wood.

Grill Roasting: cooking food at 325 to 375°F (170 to 190°C), using direct heat and charcoal/wood.

COOKERS

We've owned and operated many different types of smokers over the years, from homemade barrel cookers to $15,000 trailer rigs, and there have been plenty of times when our food has been just as amazing coming off our inexpensive equipment as it was from our custom piece. In order to cook great barbecue,

you don't need fancy equipment. The pitmaster is always more important than the pit.

Following is an introduction to the kinds of equipment best suited to cooking barbecue, and a primer on getting started with all three styles.

VERTICAL SMOKERS

In the design of all vertical smokers, the charcoal fire sits directly beneath the grates holding the food being cooked. Generally, a water pan or metal plate acts as a heat buffer between the fire and meat, and allows for indirect cooking. Airflow is restricted by adjustable vents, to allow the charcoal and wood to burn steady and slow.

The gold standard of inexpensive, highly functional vertical cookers is the Weber Smokey Mountain (WSM). On the competition trail, this $300 cooker is often used to kick the butt of teams with $10,000 rigs. Numerous other smoker manufacturers that follow this basic design include the popular (but more expensive) Big Green Egg, Backwoods Smokers, and Spicewine Ironworks, to name a few. We have even seen people make these smokers out of refrigerators and metal trash barrels.

To get started with a vertical smoker:

1. Clean it. Remove any ash or old charcoal from inside the smoker.

2. If your smoker does not have a built-in thermometer, place a probe or an oven thermometer on the grill grate (see Equipment, page 20).

3. Fill the charcoal area almost to capacity with unlit lump charcoal.

4. Outside the smoker, fill a charcoal chimney with hardwood lump charcoal, crumple two pieces of newspaper and stuff them below the coals (a reason to keep subscribing to your local daily), and light the newspaper. Wait about 10 minutes for the charcoal to become fully ignited. Flames should just be starting to peek through the top of the pile.

5. Carefully, wearing heat-proof gloves, pour the lit charcoal evenly over the bed of unlit charcoal inside the smoker.

6. Fill the water pan with cold water.

7. Depending on the type of vertical smoker you are using, either close the doors or cover with the smoker lid. Open the top and bottom vents completely.

8. When the temperature inside the smoker reaches 250°F (120°C), remove the lid and clean the grill grates with a brush. If your recipe calls for it, now is the time to add what is known as the "smoke wood"—usually two or three fist-sized chunks of dry hardwood such as apple, cherry, oak, or hickory.

9. Close the smoker and let it return to the target temperature your recipe calls for.

10. Add the food to be cooked, and allow the smoker to return to the target temperature.

11. Close the bottom vents by three-quarters.

12. Adjust the bottom vents to maintain the temperature. Close them slightly to lower the temperature; open them slightly to raise the temperature.

13. If the temperature runs too hot, close the top vent by half. This will bring the temperature down.

14. Add water to the water pan every 3 to 4 hours. You don't ever want it to run dry.

15. A full load of charcoal should be enough fuel for most cooking sessions. But keep an eye on how much charcoal is being used and add more as needed to maintain your target temperature.

OFFSET SMOKERS

Offset smokers feature a long horizontal cooking chamber sitting next to a firebox. These range from a small $500 model available at hardware stores (our first smoker, which we don't recommend) to enormous, heavy steel models costing upwards of $15,000. Typically, these latter constructions are custom-made in the southern United States, like the Jambo Pit we use in competition.

Whereas vertical smokers use predominantly hardwood lump charcoal, offset smokers take a base of charcoal but are primarily fueled by wood logs. And while the airflow is constrained in vertical smokers, the offset smoker depends on powerful airflow to keep a log fire burning and to heat up all that steel.

The offset smoker provides a simpler, more primal, hands-on approach to smoking food. While vertical smokers can be left unattended for several hours, their offset counterparts require babysitting and playing with fire—which we think is a good thing. It gives us a good excuse to sit in our lawn chairs with a cooler of beer.

To get started with an offset smoker:

1. Clean out all the ash from the firebox.

2. If your smoker does not have a built-in thermometer, place a probe or an oven thermometer on the grill grate (see Equipment, page 20).

3. Create a base of lump charcoal and pour a chimney of lit charcoal (see Vertical Smokers, page 15, for directions) into the firebox.

4. Place three splits of dry firewood over the charcoal fire, stacked like a tepee. Close the firebox door only when the wood is actively burning.

5. Once the temperature inside the smoker reaches 250°F (120°C), open the doors and clean the grill grates with a brush.

6. Add the food to be cooked and let the smoker return to the temperature indicated in the recipe.

7. Ideally, you should keep all vents completely open and control the temperature of your pit with the size of the fire. If the smoker is running too hot, you can close down the vents temporarily, but try to keep the vents completely open as much of the time as possible to promote good airflow and prevent the buildup of bitter-tasting creosote.

8. Add a new log roughly every hour to maintain a steady temperature and a good base of coals. If the fire burns down too much, add more lump charcoal to rebuild your base, then add another log.

KETTLE GRILLS

Kettle grills are probably the most common piece of charcoal-fired outdoor cooking equipment. You can cook almost all the recipes in this book with a 22-inch (55-cm) kettle grill. There are many ways to use them. For both grill roasting (see sidebar) and smoking, we prefer the two-zone fire approach, in which you build a fire on one side of the kettle. This allows for grilling close to the fire and gives the pitmaster the flexibility to move the food to the cooler side of the grill to finish cooking, if needed.

To get started:

1. Pour some hardwood lump charcoal so it piles up against one side of the kettle.

GRILL ROASTING

TO US, GRILLING (AS OPPOSED TO SMOKING) MEANS COOKING OVER DIRECT, HIGH, DRY HEAT CREATED BY BURNING CHARCOAL OR WOOD. YOU CAN GET NEARLY THE SAME RESULTS USING GAS, BUT WE PREFER THE OLD-FASHIONED WAY. AS A RULE, ITEMS THAT YIELD THE BEST RESULTS FROM GRILLING ARE THOSE THAT COOK QUICKLY, LIKE VEGETABLES, STEAKS, HOT DOGS, AND MOST FISH. THOUGH ELEMENTS OF LIVE-FIRE COOKING HAVE CHANGED OVER THE YEARS, WE ESSENTIALLY USE THE SAME METHODS THAT OUR PREHISTORIC RELATIVES FAVORED.

WE BELIEVE THERE ARE MANY FACTORS THAT CONTRIBUTE TO THE REASONS PEOPLE LOVE TO COOK OVER FIRE. SOME ARE EMOTIONAL, AND EVOKE A MEMORY OF GOOD TIMES. WE'VE ALWAYS LOVED THE SMELL OF CHARCOAL BRIQUETTES WAFTING THROUGH WARM JULY NIGHTS. BUT THERE IS ANOTHER REASON WE ALL LOVE GRILLED ITEMS—GRILLING IS ONE OF THE BEST WAYS TO ACHIEVE THE MAILLARD REACTION, NAMED AFTER THE FRENCH CHEMIST LOUIS MAILLARD. HE DISCOVERED THAT AMINO ACIDS AND SUGARS START TO CARAMELIZE AT AROUND 310°F (155°C), WHICH CAUSES A CHANGE IN THE FLAVOR OF THE FOODS BEING COOKED AND YIELDS AN ENTICING, ROASTED AROMA. WHEN COOKING LARGER CUTS, LIKE PORK LOIN, WE USE A TECHNIQUE WE CALL GRILL ROASTING THAT ALLOWS US TO DEVELOP THAT MAILLARD REACTION.

THERE IS SCIENCE INVOLVED, BUT GRILL ROASTING IS AN ART. THE EXACT RIGHT SPOT TO PLACE THE MEAT IS A CONSTANTLY MOVING TARGET. WE TRY TO GET IT AS CLOSE TO THE FIRE AS NECESSARY TO DEVELOP A PERFECT CRUST, YET AVOID BURNING IT. DEPENDING ON WHAT YOU ARE GRILL ROASTING, HOW MUCH COAL YOU HAVE, AND HOW HOT THE FIRE IS, YOU WILL NEED TO WATCH THE FOOD CLOSELY TO SEE HOW QUICKLY IT IS BROWNING, AS WELL AS CHECK THE TEMPERATURE WITH AN INTERNAL THERMOMETER.

SOMETIMES WE COVER THE GRILL IN ORDER TO GRILL ROAST. SMALLER ITEMS, LIKE LAMB CHOPS, PROBABLY DON'T NEED TO BE COOKED COVERED. BUT ITEMS THAT TAKE LONGER TO COOK, LIKE PORK LOINS AND WHOLE CHICKENS, WILL BENEFIT FROM ROASTING IN AN ENVIRONMENT THAT IS CLOSER TO AN OVEN. AS YOU BECOME MORE EXPERIENCED, FINDING THAT WONDERFUL BALANCE OF GRILLED CARAMELIZATION AND JUICY TENDER MEAT WILL COME MORE NATURALLY—AND MORE FREQUENTLY.

2. For grill roasting, fill the chimney with char-coal. For smoking, fill the chimney half-full. Use crumpled newspaper to get the fire started (see Vertical Smokers, page 15, for directions).

3. Pour the lit charcoal over the pile of unlit charcoal. One side of the grill should now have an active charcoal fire going and the other side should have no charcoal at all.

4. For grill roasting, open the lid and place the food on the grate close to the fire. Once it has been seared and crusted on all sides, move to the cooler side of the grill. Cover the grill, and let the food finish cooking until it reaches the desired internal temperature. This method allows for getting a great sear while also cook-ing a thick cut through without burning the exterior.

5. For smoking, open the lid and remove the grill grate. Place a couple chunks of wood on the fire and a disposable aluminum pan next to the fire. Replace the grill grate and place the meat directly over the drip pan. Close the lid and position the exhaust vent away from the fire so the smoke is drawn across and over the meat. Adjust the bottom vents so they are three-quarters closed. Add more charcoal every 1 to 2 hours, rotating the meat to ensure even cooking.

GAS GRILLS

As a general rule, we do not recommend gas grills. If you are interested in starting to barbecue for a mini-mal investment, you should be able to find a decent used kettle grill at a yard sale. However, in a pinch, you can make a gas grill work. Buy some wood chips and soak them in water for an hour. Then wrap them tightly in a pouch of heavy-duty aluminum foil, and prick a couple of small holes in the foil. Turn on the grill and run a two-zone fire, with one side of the grill set at medium-high and the other side turned off. Place the wood packet directly on the lit gas element. Cook meats on the side of the grill that is turned off. For larger cuts, add a second packet of wood chips after a couple of hours.

GENERAL TIPS FOR SUCCESS

• Calibrate your thermometer. Fill a glass with ice water. Submerge the tip of the thermometer in the water. It should read 32°F (0°C). If it doesn't, adjust it according to the manufactur-er's instructions. Or treat yourself to a new thermometer.

• Monitor the grate temperature of the cooker with a calibrated probe thermometer. Temperatures can vary quite a bit from the grate to the exhaust, so always monitor the tem-peratures close to the foods you are smoking.

• Never use lighter fluid—unless you want your food to taste like gasoline.

- Charcoal chimneys rule—to light one, place the chimney on top of your grill grate, or in another spot that has good airflow from below and is fire-safe. Crumple two sheets of newspaper and stuff into the bottom of the chimney. Add charcoal to the top of the chimney. Light the newspaper in three or four spots. Five to ten minutes later, the charcoal should be lit and ready to transfer to smoker or grill.

- Burn a clean fire. This will produce sweet smoke flavor and more of a ruby red color on the meats. You know you have a clean fire when all you can see coming out of the exhaust is a thin blue line of smoke. White, billowing puffs of smoke mean you are not ready to cook yet. Black smoke means your smoker is not clean—or your food is on fire.

- Make sure your wood supply is dry and has been aged for at least six months. It should burn easily and not smolder.

- Don't soak wood in water (unless you're adapting a gas grill for smoking). Wet wood will smolder and the fire will not burn clean. Good airflow that allows the chunks of wood to actively combust instead of smolder is key. Without active combustion, creosote forms. This thick, oily substance produces a bitter flavor and dark, burnt-looking meats.

- When getting started, err on the side of using not enough smoke wood, rather than too much. Later, when you have more experience, you can add more to suit your taste. We find guests and judges enjoy a mild hint of smoke that does not dominate the flavor of the food.

- Only close the top exhaust vent to lower the temperature if you overshoot the target significantly for what you are cooking. Otherwise, the top vent should remain completely open, which encourages a clean fire.

- Small, inexpensive offset cookers typically don't have strong enough airflow to burn a clean fire using wood logs. Try using a mixture of one-quarter wood logs and three-quarters charcoal instead.

- Be patient when adjusting vents to change the cooker temperature. Make small tweaks and wait 20 to 30 minutes to check the results. If the temperature is still not quite where you need it to be, make another adjustment. Temperature changes should be slow and steady, without spikes.

- Some cooks use alternatives to water to act as a heat buffer. One option that works well is filling the water pan with sand, then covering the entire pan with aluminum foil. Some smoker manufacturers use ceramic or metal plates to act as a heat shield.

- Some recipes in this book call for higher temperatures than those commonly used in a smoker. In order to hit the 300 to 400°F (150 to 200°C) range using a vertical smoker, we suggest running it with an empty water pan. Make sure the pan is very clean, and line it with foil to make cleanup easy. For an offset smoker, build up a significant base of coals and get three or four logs burning. Keep the door of your smoker open until the fire is fully engaged.

- Make sure grill grates are clean so food won't stick. It's easier to clean them when they are hot, so heat the smoker before you start. Once the grates are warm, wearing heat-proof gloves, brush them with a stiff wire brush to remove any debris from previous cooking.

- Prepare for long smoking sessions. Pork butt and brisket recipes in this book call for 8- to 10-hour cooking times. If you are planning to take these meats fresh off the smoker for an afternoon party or competition turn-in, you will need to cook overnight. If you are using a vertical smoker, load up the charcoal area with as much as you can fit. From there, make sure you have enough charcoal on hand for refueling and access to water for replenishing the water pan if you are using one. The last thing you want to be doing at four o'clock in the morning is searching around your garage for that bag of charcoal. If you are using an offset smoker, you'll need someone to babysit the fire. Our IQUE teammate Jamie Hart is renowned for late-night poker playing while keeping a steady fire into the wee hours.

EQUIPMENT

THERMOMETERS

Probe thermometer—These nifty little devices let you monitor the air temperature in your smoker and the food temperature without having to open the cooker.

Thermapen—This is a pocket-sized, instant-read thermometer that will give you the temperature of your food immediately.

Draft control systems—These small, computerized systems monitor the pit temperature and automatically fan the fire to keep the temperature steady. Draft controls work best for vertical smokers that have a tight fit and low airflow. Our favorite is from the BBQ Guru and allows us to get a few hours of sleep at contests or during overnight cooking sessions at home without having to watch the smoker. Don't forget, though, you still need to keep that water pan full!

Marinade injector—Several of our recipes call for injecting marinade into the meat because traditional marinades will not penetrate thick cuts, like pork butt. A marinade injector allows us to quickly add flavor to the inner parts of the meat. They range in price from $5 plastic to $50 stainless steel models. We prefer the cheap ones, which we treat almost as disposable after a few uses. If you have an expensive model, be sure to clean it thoroughly after every use.

Stainless steel tongs—We keep 10-, 12-, and 16-inch (25-, 30-, and 40-cm) models on hand. Longer tongs are great for adjusting a fire or adding wood chunks, where smaller tongs are perfect for flipping meats on the grill. Always use tongs to flip meats; never pierce meats with a fork, which allows the juices to escape.

Gloves—When you play with fire, things are gonna get hot. We recommend having a good pair of heat-proof gloves around at all times, both to move hot meats around on the grate, and for when you're transferring coals from the charcoal chimney to your smoker or grill. It's also a good idea to have food-handling gloves, for working with raw meat, and sometimes even the cooked stuff—like pulled pork.

Cleaning brushes—Keep a variety of grill brushes on hand. Burnt carbonized bits of food stuck to the grate from your last cooking session definitely do not improve flavor.

Charcoal chimney starter—This is a must-have tool. With a chimney, which you fill with coals, then light newspaper to start the fire, you will never have to use lighter fluid again.

CHARCOAL AND WOOD

Hardwood lump—Though most people grew up with the pressure-treated charcoal briquettes, hardwood lump charcoal is the real deal and, as far as we're concerned, usually the way to go. It burns cleaner than briquettes, with less ash. Not all lump charcoal is created equal. Some is made from kiln-dried lumber scraps that burn very quickly. Seek out dense hardwood charcoal; our favorite is Wicked Good Charcoal (no relation).

Briquettes—These are usually treated with chemicals and have more ash, though there are some hardwood briquettes. One of the benefits of briquettes is their uniform shape. This means you can fit more fuel in your firebox and do not need to replenish it as often. If you must use briquettes, make sure they are natural, with a starch binder and no chemical additives.

Smoke woods—Our favorites are apple, cherry, oak, hickory, pecan, and guava. The smoke wood should be dry and seasoned, but never kiln-dried. In vertical smokers, throw on a chunk to give your food extra flavor. In offset smokers, it is the primary source of heat as well.

CHAPTER 2

TAKING HOME THE PRIZE

HOW A GROUP OF FRIENDS FROM THE NORTH WON THE WORLD CHAMPIONSHIP OF BARBECUE

GRAND CHAMPION
21ST ANNUAL
JACK DANIEL'S ®
WORLD CHAMPIONSHIP INVITATIONAL BARBECUE
Lynchburg, Tennessee

MAKING GOOD BARBECUE in your backyard is relatively easy. Food generally tastes better cooked over fire, and with judicious use of rubs, marinades, and sauces, you can elevate meat, chicken, and fish to something special. But getting to the level of winning barbecue championships—let alone THE world championship—is a whole different animal.

While we had a lot of fun from the beginning, there were three years of mediocre results between our first competition and our first state championship. Leading up to that win, Chris spent hours and hours, weekend after weekend, year after year in his backyard, testing and refining recipes. He made so much brisket that his next-door neighbor's dog refused to eat any more. His wife and kids went on a barbecue strike. They wouldn't touch any meat or chicken that had even a hint of smoke. But his hard work paid off.

Now, when that sweet smoky scent wafts through his neighborhood, word spreads through town and people start flocking. By this point, most of them know what they'll be getting. But occasionally, somebody will wander in who has never experienced competition-style barbecue. After one taste, in Chris's words, "they go nuts."

But there's no resting on our laurels. Chris and the rest of the IQUE team work as hard as ever to maintain the quality of our barbecue. The difference between now and the early days is knowing that the food will be consistently great because of our years of practice and repetition. It's kind of like shooting free throws. When you start you may get one out of every ten. The next month, if you've been practicing every day, several hours a day, maybe three out of ten go in. A few years later, you're up there with Ray Allen (hey, we're from Boston).

We know the recipes in this chapter are intense. They're long. There's a lot to read. But if you want to be the best barbecue person on your block, the best barbecue person in your neighborhood, the best barbecue person in your state, or on your competition circuit, you need more than a little intensity. Which does not preclude fun. We wouldn't be doing any of this if it weren't fun. And neither should you.

This chapter covers what are known in barbecue competitions as the Four Mains—chicken, ribs, pork, and brisket. The first time you make the recipes, your results will be delicious. Everybody who tastes them will be blown away. The second time, the results will be even better. And you'll build from there.

So sit down, grab a beer, and read this chapter. Then get outside and start smoking.

★ 25-STEP CHAMPIONSHIP CHICKEN ★

12 meaty chicken thighs, about 5 pounds (2.27 kg) total (preferably hormone- and antibiotic-free, with no added water or other solutions)

½ cup (64 g) Activa Transglutaminase (Meat Glue), optional (see Resources, page 218)

1½ cups (355 ml) low-sodium chicken broth

1 cup (200 g) White BBQ Rub (recipe follows)

¾ cup (1½ sticks, 167 g) margarine (do not substitute butter)

2 cups (475 ml) IQUE BBQ Sauce (page 35)

1 cup (235 ml) white grape juice

¾ cup (175 ml) agave nectar

SPECIAL EQUIPMENT:

2 disposable aluminum pans (approximately 10 × 12 inches, or 25 × 30 cm), marinade injector

We don't call this "championship" chicken for nothing. We've won a lot of prizes with this recipe. We've included instructions for trimming thighs to precise, uniform proportions, a basic requirement for competition. IQUE teammate Dave Frary is an expert at this. If you would rather just focus on the flavor, you can simply trim excess fat and skin from each thigh with a pair of kitchen shears.

Using a sharp knife, cut skin off each thigh in one piece, being careful not to tear the skin. Reserve skin pieces.

Lay thighs side-by-side on a cutting board, and trim each one into uniform, trapezoid shapes (A).

Turn thighs over and cut away muscle along the back of the thigh bone.

Scrape excess fat off edges of chicken skin. Don't remove all the fat from the thigh, just the excess chunks. The fat provides moisture and flavor, so you want to leave some.

Trim skins so they are slightly smaller than the thighs. The skin should wrap around the thigh, fully covering the front and about half of the back. You'll need to keep a small area of meat exposed on the back of the thigh for seasoning.

Reattach the skin to the thigh using one of the following methods:

✪ Meat glue method—Sprinkle about 1 teaspoon meat glue on the inside of each piece of skin (B). Place the thigh front-side down on the skin and wrap the skin around the thigh (C). Wrap tightly in plastic wrap, or vacuum seal, and refrigerate for 4 hours or overnight.

✪ Toothpick method: Using four toothpicks, fasten the skin to the thigh, and refrigerate for 4 hours or overnight.

A: TRIM CHICKEN THIGHS INTO UNIFORM PIECES.

B: SPRINKLE MEAT GLUE ONTO THE INSIDE OF EACH PIECE OF SKIN.

C: REWRAPPED THIGHS, READY TO BE REFRIGERATED.

25-STEP CHAMPIONSHIP CHICKEN (CONTINUED)

Place the thighs skin-side down in a baking pan large enough to hold them in a single layer. Using a marinade injector, inject ½ ounce (14 ml) chicken broth into the meat on the left and the right sides of each thigh bone, for a total of 1 ounce (28 ml) per thigh. It is easiest to inject aiming down from the top of the thigh. Dry completely with paper towels. Sprinkle about ½ tablespoon (3.9 g) White BBQ Rub on the back of each thigh, and let sit at room temperature for 20 minutes.

Prepare smoker and bring temperature to 250 to 275°F (120 to 140°C). Use a mild wood such as apple.

Sprinkle about ½ tablespoon (3.9 g) White BBQ Rub on the front of each thigh.

Place 6 tablespoons (85 g) margarine in each aluminum pan. Lay one thigh skin-side up on each pat of margarine.

When smoker is ready, put both pans in and close lid. Smoke for 1 hour.

Remove pans from smoker and cover tightly with aluminum foil to tenderize the skin. Return pans to smoker for 1 hour.

In a medium saucepan over medium heat, stir together IQUE BBQ Sauce and white grape juice. Reduce heat to low and keep warm, stirring occasionally.

Remove thighs from the smoker. If skin is attached to meat with toothpicks, remove them. Using tongs or gloved hands, submerge each piece into the warm BBQ Sauce mixture. Shake off the excess, then transfer to a foil-lined baking sheet or disposable aluminum pan.

Again using tongs or gloved hands, lay each thigh directly on the smoker grate. The smoker temperature should be unchanged. Smoke for 20 to 30 minutes, to allow the sauce to caramelize.

Spread out a 16-inch (40-cm) piece of aluminum foil. Squirt 12 swirls of agave nectar on the foil. Sprinkle a pinch of White BBQ Rub onto each swirl. Remove thighs from the smoker and place each one on a swirl. Sprinkle another pinch of White BBQ Rub onto each thigh and let rest for 10 minutes. Get ready for a perfect score.

YIELD: 12 servings

WHITE BBQ RUB

½ cup (150 g) kosher salt

6 tablespoons (69 g) turbinado sugar

3 tablespoons (18 g) freshly ground white pepper

4 teaspoons (8 g) lemon pepper

4 teaspoons (12 g) garlic powder

2 teaspoons (4.8 g) onion powder

2 teaspoons (9.2 g) powdered citric acid

1 teaspoon (3 g) dry mustard

Mix all ingredients thoroughly, then process in batches in a spice grinder to a fine powder. Store in an airtight container for up to 1 month.

YIELD: 1½ cups (150 g)

MEAT GLUE

TRANSGLUTAMINASE IS AN ENZYME THAT OCCURS NATURALLY IN PLANTS, ANIMALS, AND BACTERIA. KNOWN IN FOOD PRODUCTION AND TO CHEFS AS MEAT GLUE, IT BONDS PROTEINS TOGETHER, LIKE TWO PIECES OF RAW MEAT, OR MEAT MIXTURES LIKE SAUSAGES WITHOUT CASINGS. WE LIKE TO USE IT TO HOLD OUR CHICKEN SKIN IN PLACE, SO IT DOESN'T END UP ON THE CHIN OF A BARBECUE JUDGE. BUT USE IT WITH CAUTION. LIKE ANY POWDER, YOU SHOULD TRY TO AVOID INHALING IT. IF YOU GET IT IN YOUR EYES, FLUSH IT OUT WITH PLENTY OF WATER; ON YOUR SKIN, WASH WITH SOAP AND WATER. BUT DON'T WORRY—IT WON'T BIND YOUR FINGERS TOGETHER LIKE SAUSAGES.

★ THE RIBS THAT WON ★
THE JACK DANIEL'S WORLD CHAMPIONSHIP

2 racks untrimmed pork spare ribs (about 5 pounds, or 2.27 kg, each)

2 tablespoons (30 ml) Butcher BBQ Pork Marinade Injection, optional (see Resources, page 218)

½ cup (120 ml) water, optional

1 cup (100 g) IQUE Dry Rub (recipe follows)

1 cup (150 g) Brownulated light brown sugar

1 cup (235 ml) amber agave nectar

2 tablespoons (13.8 g) onion powder

1 cup (235 ml) Pork Marinade Sauce (recipe follows)

1 cup (235 ml) IQUE BBQ Sauce (recipe follows)

Being a couple of guys from New England, going down into the heart of barbecue country and winning the Jack Daniel's World Championship was a thrill of a lifetime. In order to cook ribs that win big, you need extreme attention to detail. You're going for a bold flavor that will get the judges' attention in one bite. When you're up against ninety-five of the best barbecue cooks in the world, you'd better stand out. Why do any less when you're cooking at home?

For these ribs, we like to trim the racks into what is called a St. Louis cut because it highlights the prime part of the rib bone. Any butcher will do it, but we prefer to do it ourselves because we don't trust anybody else to cut them exactly the right way. So you can be a wimp and have someone cut your meat for you, or you can do it yourself and make sure the ribs are trimmed perfectly.

Start with large, meaty ribs with no shiners (shiners are where the butcher has cut away too much meat, so the bones "shine" through). To trim ribs to a St. Louis cut, start by placing the rack meat-side down on the cutting board. The spot where the rib bones end and the sternum and cartilage portion begins is often referred to as rib tips. Cut along the length of the ribs, removing the rib tip portion and leaving about 1 inch (2.5 cm) of meat along the edge of the rib bones (A). Be careful not to cut too close to the bone. You are looking to create a square, uniform slab of ribs. Using a very sharp chef's knife, remove the flap of meat on the back of the rack (B). With a paper towel, carefully peel the membrane off of the ribs (C).

A: CUT ALONG THE LENGTH OF THE RIBS, REMOVING THE TIP PORTION.

B: REMOVE THE FLAP OF MEAT ON THE BACK OF THE RACK.

C: USING A PAPER TOWEL, PEEL THE MEMBRANE FROM THE BACK OF THE RIBS.

THE RIBS THAT WON THE JACK DANIEL'S WORLD CHAMPIONSHIP (CONTINUED)

If using the marinade injection, mix it with water, stirring until the powder is completely dissolved. The marinade can be prepared a day in advance and refrigerated. Use marinade injector (see Equipment, page 20) to inject ½ ounce (14 ml) of the marinade between each rib bone. Start from the top of the rib, where the meat is a bit thinner. Refrigerate overnight or for at least 2 hours before smoking.

Prepare smoker and bring heat to 250 to 275°F (120 to 140°C). We recommend fruit woods, such as apple, cherry, or guava. When you see a thin, blue smoke, barely visible, coming out of your smoker, you'll know it's ready.

In the meantime, rub the ribs. Pat them dry with paper towels and lightly sprinkle front and back with IQUE Dry Rub, making sure it is spread evenly. A spice shaker works well for this, or you can just pick up some rub with your hands and sprinkle it. After the rub is applied, press the spices into the meat with gloved hands. Don't rub ribs more than an hour before they go onto the grill. If the rub sits any longer than that, it will draw moisture from the ribs and could create a hammy flavor.

Remember to clean your grill grate immaculately. When the fire is ready, add two chunks of the smoke wood and put the ribs on the smoker, meat-side up. Smoke for 2 hours. Don't open the lid of the smoker. If you're looking, you ain't cooking.

After 2 hours, flip the ribs meat-side down, using tongs or your gloved hands. If your grill grates are not immaculately clean as you flip the ribs, place a piece of foil on the grill and place the ribs on top. Smoke for 1 hour more.

Prepare ingredients for wrapping the ribs. It's important to conduct this step quickly so the ribs don't cool down. Have handy:

- Two large pieces of heavy-duty aluminum foil
- Brown sugar, agave nectar, onion powder, and Pork Marinade Sauce

Remove the ribs from the smoker. Across the length of each piece of foil, sprinkle ¼ cup (37.5 g) brown sugar and 4 tablespoons (60 ml) agave nectar. Place ribs meat-side down on the sugar. Repeat the same proportions of brown sugar and agave nectar on the back of the ribs, then pour ½ cup (120 g) Pork Marinade Sauce and sprinkle 1 tablespoon (6.9 g) onion powder on each rack. Wrap the ribs very tightly with the foil, making sure there are no air pockets. You don't want to create steam in the wrapped rib packages. If the rib bones break a hole in the foil during this process, be sure to double up with a second piece of foil.

As you are wrapping the ribs, check them for doneness. Ribs have different fat content and weights, so they will cook slightly differently. If the ribs feel like they will break apart if picked up at the center, they are close to done. Reduce the smoker to 225°F (110°C). If the ribs are still very stiff, turn the smoker up to 275°F (140°C). Return ribs to cook for another hour.

Shortly before removing ribs, bring the IQUE BBQ Sauce to a simmer and keep warm.

Remove the ribs from the cooker and check for doneness. A few of the bones should be starting to break through the meat on the back side of the ribs. If necessary, return to the smoker for an additional half hour until they reach that point. When the ribs are done, baste them with the warm barbecue sauce. Turn them over and baste the other side with the sauce. Sprinkle the meat side of each rib rack with 1 tablespoon (6 g) IQUE Dry Rub (D). Rewrap the ribs with a fresh sheet of foil and rest at room temperature, meat-side up, for 30 minutes. Remove from foil and set meat down on a clean cutting board. Carefully, slice evenly between each rib bone (E).

To serve, arrange on a large platter, with a bowl of warm IQUE BBQ Sauce on the side (F).

YIELD: 4 to 6 servings

D: SPRINKLE THE SMOKED RIBS WITH IQUE DRY RUB.

E: CAREFULLY SLICE BETWEEN EACH RIB BONE.

F: PRESENTATION READY.

IQUE DRY RUB 〉

1 cup (150 g) turbinado sugar

¾ cup (225 g) kosher salt

½ cup (56 g) high-quality paprika
(we like Spanish paprika)

6 tablespoons (45 g) chili powder

2 tablespoons (12 g) cumin seeds, freshly ground

4 teaspoons (6.8 g) mixed peppercorns,
freshly ground

4 teaspoons (12 g) garlic granules

3 teaspoons (7.2 g) onion granules

2 teaspoons (9.2 g) MSG (or Accent), optional

1 teaspoon (2.6 g) chipotle powder

Turbinado is raw sugar with coarse, blond-colored crystals. It has a light, molasses flavor. It is essential in this rub because it doesn't burn as easily as white or brown sugar. We like to use mixed peppercorns—white, black, pink, and green—because they add complex flavors, hitting different points on your tongue as you eat. Also, look for fresh chili powder, such as Gebhardt's, and paprika, which have superior flavor. They can be difficult to find at traditional grocery stores. We order ours online (see Resources, page 218), but if there is a good spice shop in your neighborhood, that is another option.

Place all ingredients in a spice blender and pulse until it becomes a fine powder. Refrigerate in an airtight container. This rub will keep indefinitely, but try to use within 1 month to ensure freshest flavor.

YIELD: 3 cups (300 g)

PORK MARINADE SAUCE

1 cup (235 ml) white grape juice

½ cup (120 ml) cider vinegar

½ cup (115 g) packed light brown sugar

¼ cup (60 ml) Worcestershire sauce

¾ cup (175 ml) IQUE BBQ Sauce (page 35)

In a small saucepan over medium heat, bring all ingredients to a simmer. Use immediately or let cool and refrigerate.

YIELD: 3 cups (750 ml)

CHARACTERISTICS OF A SUCCESSFUL COOK

IN THE BARBECUE WORLD, WHEN WE TALK ABOUT A "SUCCESSFUL COOK," WE ARE REFER-
RING TO THE END PRODUCT, RATHER THAN THE PERSON RESPONSIBLE—THOUGH IF YOU
ARE THAT PERSON, FEEL FREE TO TAKE CREDIT. THAT BEING SAID, ITS CHARACTERISTICS
INCLUDE A LIGHT, BUT NOT OVERPOWERING SMOKE FLAVOR; MEAT THAT IS TENDER BUT
NOT FALLING OFF THE BONE; JUICY, WITH A LITTLE SWEAT ON THE BONE; AND VERY SWEET
(THE JUDGES LOVE SWEET) BUT BALANCED BY THE SAVORY FLAVORS OF THE DRY RUB,
SMOKE, AND ONION.

‹ IQUE BBQ SAUCE

4 cups (600 g) packed brown sugar

1½ cups (355 ml) cider vinegar

½ cup (120 ml) Worcestershire sauce

1 tablespoon (4.8 g) dried thyme

1 tablespoon (1.6 g) ground mustard

1 tablespoon (9 g) garlic powder

1 tablespoon (7 g) ground cumin

1½ teaspoons (3 g) Szechuan peppercorns,*
freshly ground

1½ teaspoons (3 g) long peppercorns,*
freshly ground

1½ teaspoons (3.9 g) chipotle powder or cayenne
pepper

1 tablespoon (6.3 g) tomato powder,** optional

½ tablespoon (3 g) hickory powder,** optional

4 cups (946 ml) ketchup

½ cup (120 ml) light corn syrup

2 tablespoons (15 g) IQUE Dry Rub (page 32)

We like to start our sauce base with a mixture known as a gastrique—basically a sugar and vinegar reduction. It's a great way to infuse additional flavors into a sauce while maintaining a fresh, bright quality. Often, we find a long-cooking barbecue sauce can mute some of the complexity that various dry spices bring to the party. This sauce comes together in about an hour and will keep in the refrigerator for up to 1 month.

In a medium saucepan over medium-high heat, make the gastrique by bringing the brown sugar, cider vinegar, and Worcestershire sauce to a gentle boil.

Remove from heat and add the thyme, mustard, garlic powder, cumin, ground Szechuan peppercorns, ground long peppercorns, chipotle powder, and tomato powder and hickory powder, if using. Let sit for 15 minutes.

Stir in ketchup and corn syrup, return to stove, and simmer over low heat for 30 minutes. Remove from heat and add IQUE Dry Rub. Let cool and store in refrigerator, preferably in squeeze bottles, for up to 1 month.

YIELD: About 2 quarts (1.9 L)

* A blend of mixed peppercorns can be substituted for the Szechuan and long peppercorns, but in our opinion the sauce won't be nearly as wicked.

** Tomato powder and hickory powder are available by mail order or at specialty foods stores. See Resources, page 218.

★ WICKED PULLED PORK ★

FOR PULLED PORK:

2 bone-in pork butts (8 pounds, or 4 kg, each), untrimmed

2¼ cups (535 ml) Savory Pork Marinade Injection (recipe follows)

1 cup (100 g) IQUE Dry Rub (page 32)

2 cups (475 ml) IQUE BBQ Sauce, warmed (page 35)

2 cups (475 ml) Pork Marinade Sauce (page 32)

FOR SANDWICHES:

Spicy Lexington Red Slaw (recipe follows)

North Carolina Creamy Vinegar Dressing (recipe follows)

Bacon Bit Buns (recipe follows)

SPECIAL EQUIPMENT:

Marinade injector, heavy-duty aluminum foil, two 9-inch-square (22.5-cm) baking pans or disposable aluminum half-pans, food-handling gloves

Pulled pork sandwiches are a roadside barbecue staple, and one of our favorite things. Here we stay true to the tradition but elevate the sandwich to another level. Unlike most in the genre, ours combines chopped meat with beautiful, sliced pork from what is known as the "money muscle." And because there's no such thing as too much pork, Chris decided one day to add bacon bits to the rolls—an experimental move that proved to be a keeper.

Vinegar is intrinsic to North Carolina barbecue, where we love to eat pulled pork sandwiches. We developed a vinegar dressing for ours that pays homage to the state's 'cue and complements our version of their red slaw, which is another must. We also give our meat an extra burst of flavor. Traditional marinade is a problem for a big cut like a pork butt because it may only penetrate a few inches over a 24-hour period. So we take a two-pronged approach. First, we inject a marinade into the raw meat before we start cooking to give the flavors a chance to penetrate. Second, we apply a marinade to the cooked meat. The resting pork absorbs the marinade, completing the one-two punch of flavor penetration.

This is not your standard pulled pork sandwich; this version is wicked!

To make the pulled pork: Trim the pork (see sidebar, page 41).

Using a marinade injector, slowly inject the Savory Pork Marinade Injection into each pork butt in nine evenly spaced spots. There should be about 1 ounce (28 ml) of marinade in each spot.

A: SPRINKLE BUTTS WITH IQUE DRY RUB.

B: BASTE WITH IQUE BBQ SAUCE.

C: SLICE THE MONEY MUSCLE INTO
¾-INCH (1.7-CM)-THICK SLICES.

WICKED PULLED PORK (CONTINUED)

Generously sprinkle IQUE Dry Rub all over each butt and wrap each one tightly in plastic wrap (A). Refrigerate 4 to 8 hours.

Prepare smoker for a long smoking session (see chapter 1). We recommend a mild-flavored wood, such as apple. Place butts on the smoker, fat-side up. Smoke at 250°F (120°C) for 5 hours, or until internal temperature is 165°F (74°C), keeping the lid closed. Use a probe thermometer to monitor it. Turn the meat over, baste with 1 cup (235 ml) IQUE BBQ Sauce, and smoke for 2 hours, until a ruby-red crust has formed on the exterior (B).

Remove meat from smoker, wrap each butt tightly in aluminum foil, and smoke until internal temperature is 198°F (92°C). At this stage, you can open the lid, so you can switch to a super-fast Thermapen.

Transfer each pork butt to a baking pan, fat-side up. Remove foil, and pour 1 cup (235 ml) Pork Marinade Sauce over each butt. Tent each baking pan with a new piece of foil, and let rest for 1 hour.

Transfer the butts to a cutting board. Pour off the liquid from the pan and reserve. With a very sharp knife, slice the entire money muscle off each butt and place, cut-side down, on a cutting board.

Return the butts to the baking pans and, wearing food-handling gloves, pull the meat into thumb-sized chunks. Don't process the meat too finely. You want big, bold pieces of pork. Pour back the reserved liquid and stir into the meat. Sprinkle with 1 tablespoon (6 g) IQUE Dry Rub. Taste, and add a bit more hot IQUE BBQ Sauce if you think it needs it. Cover and hold in a warm (225°F, or 110°C) oven or on your smoker.

Using a very sharp carving knife, or an electric knife, slice the money muscles into ¾-inch-thick (1.7-cm) slices (C).

To make the sandwiches: Place the pulled meat in the center of a platter and fan the sliced money muscle around it. Let your guests assemble their own sandwiches with some pulled and sliced pork, Spicy Lexington Red Slaw, a drizzle of the North Carolina Creamy Vinegar Dressing, and Bacon Bit Buns.

YIELD: 12 Servings

SAVORY PORK MARINADE INJECTION

1 cup (235 ml) white grape juice

½ cup (120 ml) cider vinegar

½ cup (120 ml) agave nectar

¼ cup (60 ml) Worcestershire sauce

¼ cup (60 ml) water

2 tablespoons (36 g) kosher salt

1 tablespoon (6.9 g) onion powder

Combine all ingredients in a small bowl and mix well. Cover and keep refrigerated for up to 1 month.

YIELD: 3 cups (750 ml)

SPICY LEXINGTON RED SLAW

1 cup (235 ml) cayenne pepper sauce, such as Frank's Red Hot Sauce

½ cup (120 ml) Worcestershire sauce

¼ cup (60 ml) cider vinegar

¼ cup (60 g) packed brown sugar

2 tablespoons (15 g) chili powder

1 head napa cabbage, thinly sliced

2 carrots, shredded

2 tablespoons (15 g) IQUE Dry Rub (page 32)

North Carolina is one of our favorite barbecue regions, and when we're in the region, Lexington BBQ #1 is one of our favorite road food stops. Pulled pork, red slaw, hushpuppies, and sweet tea is about as good as it gets. Our version of this famous slaw packs a bit more kick and pairs perfectly with our Wicked Pulled Pork.

In a small bowl over medium heat, bring cayenne pepper sauce, Worcestershire sauce, vinegar, brown sugar, and chili powder to a simmer. Lower heat and simmer gently for 30 minutes. Remove from heat and let cool to room temperature.

In a large bowl, mix cabbage, carrots, and dry rub, and toss to combine. Stir in the sauce.

We like the crunch and texture of fresh slaw best, but this will hold in an airtight container in the refrigerator for up to 1 week. Serve with Wicked Pulled Pork, or as a side dish to just about any of your favorite barbecued meats, chicken, or fish.

YIELD: 12 servings

NORTH CAROLINA
CREAMY VINEGAR DRESSING

2 eggs

1 cup (235 ml) plus 2 tablespoons (30 ml) cider vinegar

2 cups (475 ml) canola oil

1½ tablespoons (25 ml) fresh lemon juice (from ½ lemon)

2 tablespoons (30 g) Dijon mustard

1 head roasted garlic, cloves removed and mashed to a smooth paste

⅔ cup (132 g) sugar

1 tablespoon (3.6 g) crushed red pepper flakes

1 tablespoon (4 g) fresh parsley, chopped

1 tablespoon (3 g) chives, chopped

1 tablespoon (7 g) ground paprika

½ tablespoon (3 g) freshly ground black pepper

In a food processor or a blender set on medium, mix eggs and 2 tablespoons (30 ml) of the cider vinegar. With the motor running, slowly drizzle in oil until it is the consistency of jarred mayonnaise. (You may not need all of the oil.)

Add remaining 1 cup (235 ml) cider vinegar, lemon juice, mustard, garlic, sugar, and red pepper flakes, and mix for 2 to 3 minutes. Add parsley, chives, paprika, and ground pepper, and pulse the dressing a few times. Pour into a squeeze bottle and refrigerate for up to 2 weeks.

YIELD: 3 cups (750 ml)

‹ BACON BIT BUNS

1 pound (455 g) sliced bacon

3 tablespoons (22.5 g) IQUE Dry Rub (page 32)

1 cup (2 sticks, 225 g) butter, melted

2 tablespoons (30 ml) bacon fat, reserved from frying bacon

12 white hamburger buns

In a large sauté pan over medium-high heat, fry the bacon in batches until very crisp. Transfer to paper towels to drain, reserving 2 tablespoons (30 ml) bacon fat.

With a chef's knife, mince the bacon and transfer to a mixing bowl. Add IQUE Dry Rub and toss to combine.

In another bowl, stir together the melted butter and hot bacon fat.

Dip the top of a roll into the butter mixture, then sprinkle on bacon bits. Repeat with remaining roll tops and reserve at room temperature until ready to serve.

YIELD: 12 buns

FINDING THE MONEY MUSCLE

ON THE BACK SIDE OF THE PORK BUTT IS THE SHOULDER BONE, WHICH MAKES SENSE BECAUSE THIS CUT IS ACTUALLY FROM THE ANIMAL'S SHOULDER. THE MUSCLE PERPENDICULAR TO THIS BONE SPANS THE FRONT OF THE BUTT AND LOOKS LIKE A SMALL PORK TENDERLOIN. COOKS ON THE COMPETITION BARBECUE TRAIL OFTEN REFER TO THIS PIECE OF MEAT AS THE "MONEY MUSCLE" BECAUSE IT IS THE MOST SUCCULENT, TENDER PART OF THE PORK BUTT. MANY TROPHIES HAVE BEEN WON TURNING THIS PIECE IN AT BARBECUE COMPETITIONS. WE FEATURED THE MONEY MUSCLE AT THE JACK DANIEL'S WORLD CHAMPIONSHIP IN 2009 AND WON.

TO MAKE SURE THE MONEY MUSCLE WILL BE JUST RIGHT FOR YOUR PULLED PORK SANDWICHES, BEFORE SMOKING THE PORK BUTT, PLACE IT FAT-DOWN ON THE CUTTING BOARD. TRIM AWAY A LITTLE FAT AROUND THE MUSCLE. REMOVING THE FAT ALLOWS A NICE BARK TO FORM, AND YOU WILL BE ABLE TO SLICE IT SEPARATELY AFTER THE WHOLE BUTT IS COOKED.

★ THE AMERICAN ROYAL ★
1ST PLACE BEEF BRISKET

1 whole, untrimmed beef brisket, 16 to 18 pounds (7.3 to 8.2 kg)

2 cups (475 ml) Beef Marinade Injection (recipe follows)

½ cup (120 ml) Worcestershire sauce

1 cup (100 g) Beef BBQ Dry Rub (recipe follows)

½ cup (50 g) Dalmatian Rub (page 139)

¾ cup (175 ml) Beef BBQ Marinade, warmed (recipe follows)

½ cup (120 ml) IQUE BBQ Sauce (page 35)

SPECIAL EQUIPMENT:

Marinade injector, probe thermometer, heavy-duty aluminum foil, disposable aluminum roasting pan, insulated cooler

It's a big production for a group of guys from New England to travel out to Kansas City for the biggest barbecue contest in the world, the American Royal. In 2007, our plan included one definite—we were going to cook burnt ends, the cornerstone of Kansas City barbecue, for the brisket category.

Like most things barbecue, burnt ends—the fatty scraps of a brisket—started out as a throw-away piece of meat. Barbecue restaurants used to give this cut away as bar snacks. Kansas City folks grew to realize it was the tastiest part of the entire brisket. Nowadays, restaurants in this city are often judged solely on the quality of their burnt ends. With 530 competitors from all over the United States in this event, we knew it was important to cook some rocking burnt ends.

When we're cooking beef, we look for a different flavor profile than our barbecue pork recipes. This recipe shies away from sweet notes and leans more toward savory. We have created layers of flavor with multiple rubs, marinades, and injections that should yield something smoky, savory, spicy, peppery, and, above all, beefy. Yes, it's time-consuming, but in order to beat out 530 teams, the brisket needed to be bold, over the top, with lots of wow factor.

Throughout the weekend, as awards were announced in the different categories—chicken, ribs, pork, sauce, sausage, and side dishes—we never heard our name called. By the time the brisket category came up, we were looking at our last chance. With every competitor crammed into the American Royal livestock arena, eagerly listening to the results, the announcers called the top twenty. We were all on the on the edge of our seats as teams ranked number twenty through number two were called—and no IQUE. We had either traveled all the way

A: TRIM AWAY KNOB OF HARD, WHITE FAT.

B: (CONTINUED.)

C: REMOVE ANY EXCESS FAT FROM THE FLAT.

THE AMERICAN ROYAL 1ST PLACE BEEF BRISKET (CONTINUED)

from Boston to be shut out, or we had just won one of the biggest awards in barbecue. The name of this recipe should tell you all you need to know.

This recipe is perfect for a party or large gathering—or, if you're just in the mood to make it, it's a great excuse to have a party. As soon as your neighbors get a whiff of the smoke, they're sure to come around anyway.

Trim the brisket (see sidebar, page 48) (A–D).

Inject the brisket evenly throughout the point and flat (see sidebar) with Beef Marinade Injection.

Rub Worcestershire sauce all over the brisket. Generously rub top, bottom, and sides of brisket with Beef BBQ Dry Rub. Wrap tightly with plastic wrap and refrigerate for 4 to 8 hours.

Remove brisket from the plastic wrap and apply a second layer of Beef BBQ Dry Rub, then rub evenly with Dalmatian Rub. Let sit at room temperature for 30 minutes.

Prepare smoker and bring temperature to 250°F (120°F). Beef can handle a more assertive smoke, and we recommend either hickory or pecan as the smoke wood.

Place the brisket on the smoker, fat-side up, and smoke for 6 hours.

Turn the brisket over. Apply a light dusting of Beef BBQ Dry Rub to the flat (see sidebar) (E). Cook for 2 hours, or until meat's internal temperature registers approximately 170°F (77°C).

Prepare for the wrapping step. Have handy a probe thermometer, three 18-inch (45-cm) pieces of heavy-duty foil, and warm Beef BBQ Marinade.

Remove brisket from smoker. Form a "boat" with two pieces of foil. Place the brisket fat-side down into the boat (F). Insert the probe thermometer into the thickest part of the flat, in the same direction as the brisket's grain. Pour Beef BBQ Marinade over the brisket. Wrap the third piece of foil tightly around the brisket, removing as much air as possible.

Return brisket to the smoker and increase temperature inside the smoker to 275°F (140°C). Cook until the brisket's internal temperature is 200°F (93°C). This should take approximately 2 hours more, for roughly 10 hours total cooking time. Another way to gauge whether the brisket is done is to check for fork tenderness. If a fork can slide into the meat with almost no resistance, it is ready.

Remove brisket from foil and pour accumulated juices into a cup or bowl. Place the brisket fat-side up on the foil. Allow the meat to release its steam by resting for roughly 10 minutes (G). (If you don't do this, the brisket could overcook during its resting phase.) Pour the reserved marinade over the brisket and wrap tightly in foil. Place the meat in an empty cooler (with no ice), and let it rest for 2 hours.

To serve: In a small saucepan over medium heat, warm IQUE BBQ Sauce. Remove the brisket from the foil, reserving the juices. Using a sharp knife, separate the point section from the flat. Slice the point into ¾-inch (1.7-cm) cubes and place into a disposable aluminum pan. Toss with IQUE Sauce, cover with foil, and place back on the smoker for 30 minutes.

Trim some of the excess fat off the back of the flat, leaving an even ¼ inch (6 mm) of fat. Turn the brisket over and, using your slicing guide (see sidebar), carve pencil-thin slices (H). Brush each slice with the reserved marinade and sprinkle with another dusting of Beef BBQ Dry Rub (I). Fan slices on a platter, sprinkle the burnt end cubes around the edges, and serve.

YIELD: 25 servings

D: TRIMMED BRISKET, READY FOR SEASONING.

E: APPLY BEEF BBQ DRY RUB TO FLAT.

F: BRISKET IN ITS FOIL "BOAT."

G: RESTING.

H: CARVE PENCIL-THIN SLICES.

I: ANOTHER DUSTING OF BEEF BBQ
DRY RUB.

BEEF BBQ DRY RUB

½ cup (150 g) kosher salt

½ cup (64 g) paprika

¼ cup (30 g) chili powder*

2 tablespoons (12 g) cumin seeds, ground

2 tablespoons (26 g) turbinado sugar

2 tablespoons (12 g) freshly ground black pepper

1 tablespoon (6 g) freshly ground white pepper

1 tablespoon (9 g) garlic powder

1 tablespoon (6.9 g) onion powder

1 tablespoon (7.5 g) chipotle powder

½ tablespoon (3.7 g) hickory powder, optional (see Resources, page 218)

In a small bowl, combine all ingredients and mix well. Store in an airtight container for up to 1 month.

YIELD: 2 cups (200 g)

* We recommend using high-quality fresh chili powder, such as Gebhardt's, which has superior flavor. It can be difficult to find at traditional grocery stores, but you can find sources online. Other options are the custom chili blends available from Pendery's (see Resources, page 218), or any good spice shop in your neighborhood.

BEEF BBQ MARINADE

12 ounces (335 ml) American lager

1 cup (235 ml) low-sodium beef broth

1 head roasted garlic, cloves removed and processed to a paste

¼ cup (60 ml) canola oil

¼ cup (60 ml) soy sauce

¼ cup (60 ml) yellow mustard

¼ cup (25 g) Beef BBQ Dry Rub

2 tablespoons (7.2 g) crushed red pepper flakes

Place all ingredients in a mason jar or other airtight container. Cover and shake vigorously. Refrigerate for up to 1 week.

YIELD: About 3 cups (750 ml)

BEEF MARINADE INJECTION

½ cup (70 g) Butcher BBQ Brisket Injection (see Resources, page 218)

2 cups (475 ml) cold water

Or

2 cups (475 ml) low-sodium beef broth

2 beef bouillon cubes

2 tablespoons (30 ml) Worcestershire sauce

We use the first option in competition. We prefer it, but if you don't have (or don't want to get) the brisket injection, the second method works well also.

Mix Butcher BBQ Brisket Injection well with cold water.

Or

Bring beef broth to a boil with beef bouillon cubes and Worcestershire sauce. Let cool.

YIELD: 2 cups (475 ml)

BRISKET SELECTION, WET-AGE, AND TRIM INSTRUCTIONS

NOT ALL BRISKETS ARE CREATED EQUAL. COMPETITION BARBECUE COOKS SPEND QUITE A BIT OF TIME SOURCING AND SELECTING THE PERFECT BRISKET. WE ONLY USE THE WHOLE, UNTRIMMED, CRYOVAC-SEALED PACKER BRISKETS. THE WHOLE BRISKET CONTAINS BOTH THE POINT AND THE FLAT PORTIONS. OFTEN, THE SUPERMARKET SELLS ONLY THE FLAT PORTION OF THE BRISKET, WITH THE FAT REMOVED. THIS CUT IS FINE FOR POT ROAST, BUT IT WILL YIELD SOMETHING AKIN TO SHOE LEATHER IF COOKED IN A BARBECUE METHOD.

LOOK FOR BRISKETS THAT HAVE A UNIFORM 2-INCH-THICK (4.5-CM) FLAT. ONE GOLDEN RULE IS THAT IF YOU WANT AN EVENLY COOKED BRISKET, THE BRISKET HAS TO HAVE AN EVEN SHAPE. WE GENERALLY RECOMMEND SEEKING OUT A MINIMUM OF CHOICE GRADE, THOUGH WE HAVE CREATED SOME SPECTACULAR RESULTS USING PRIME GRADE BRISKETS AND EVEN AMERICAN WAGYU BEEF. WAGYU CAN GET EXPENSIVE, BUT IT HAS AN EXTRA-HIGH FAT CONTENT THAT KEEPS THE MEAT SUPER-MOIST DURING THE LONG COOKING PROCESS.

WET-AGING THE BRISKET

ONE CHALLENGE WHEN SMOKING A BRISKET IS TO GET THE MEAT TENDER WITHOUT DRYING IT OUT. AGING THE BEEF HELPS ENHANCE BOTH THE FLAVOR AND THE TENDERNESS. HIGH-END STEAKHOUSES OFTEN DRY-AGE BEEF. THE MAIN BENEFIT FROM DRY-AGING IS THAT MOISTURE EVAPORATES AND THE BEEF FLAVOR IS CONCENTRATED. THE MAIN BENEFIT OF WET-AGING FALLS MORE ON THE TENDERNESS SIDE OF THE EQUATION. WET-AGING RELEASES ENZYMES THAT HELP SOFTEN THE TOUGH CONNECTIVE TISSUES. WE HAVE FOUND THAT WET-AGING IS THE PREFERRED METHOD FOR BARBECUE BEEF BRISKET.

TO BEGIN, DETERMINE THE BRISKET'S KILL DATE, OR PACK DATE. OFTEN, THE ONLY WAY TO DETERMINE THIS IS TO BUY A CASE OF BRISKETS. THE PACK DATE WILL BE ON THE CASE. WE HIGHLY RECOMMEND BUYING A FULL CASE (ABOUT 80 POUNDS, OR 36 KG) BECAUSE YOU WILL GET A BETTER PRICE, AND YOU CAN WET-AGE ALL THE BRISKETS AT ONE TIME, THEN FREEZE SOME OF THEM FOR FUTURE USE. IT'S NICE TO KNOW YOU HAVE A WET-AGED BRISKET IN THE FREEZER WAITING FOR YOUR NEXT BARBECUE COOKING SESSION.

ONCE YOU HAVE THE PACK DATE, YOU'LL NEED A REFRIGERATOR THAT CAN MAINTAIN A CONSISTENT 35 TO 38°F (1.7 TO 3.3°C). IF IT'S TOO COLD, THE TENDERIZING ENZYMES WILL NOT RELEASE. SPIKES IN TEMPERATURE ARE NOT CONDUCIVE TO THIS TECHNIQUE, SO THE KITCHEN REFRIGERATOR, WHICH GETS A LOT OF TRAFFIC, IS NOT A GOOD CHOICE. A SECOND REFRIGERATOR IN YOUR GARAGE OR BASEMENT IS A BETTER CHOICE (UNLESS THAT'S YOUR BEER REFRIGERATOR, WHICH PROBABLY ALSO GETS A LOT OF TRAFFIC).

PLACE THE SEALED BRISKET IN THE REFRIGERATOR FOR 30 DAYS TO WET-AGE IT. IF AT ANY TIME THE CRYOVAC IS PIERCED, ALLOWING AIR TO REACH THE BRISKET, YOUR WET-AGING EXPERIMENT IS OVER. IMMEDIATELY COOK OR FREEZE THAT BRISKET. WHEN READY TO COOK THE WET-AGED BRISKET, IT'S LIKELY YOU WILL DETECT A MUSTY SMELL WHEN YOU OPEN THE CRYOVAC. RINSE THE BRISKET UNDER COLD WATER AND THE SMELL SHOULD DISSIPATE. IF A STRONG SOUR SMELL PERSISTS, THROW THE BRISKET AWAY. SPOILAGE OF THIS NATURE SHOULD NOT OCCUR IF YOU HAVE THE CORRECT PACKING DATE, KEEP YOUR REFRIGERATOR AROUND 36°F (2.2°C), AND PROTECT THE BRISKET FROM EXPOSURE TO AIR.

TRIMMING THE BRISKET (A–D)

THERE ARE TWO MAIN PARTS OF THE BRISKET, COMMONLY REFERRED TO AS THE *POINT* AND THE *FLAT*. THE FLAT IS A LEANER PORTION THAT IS TRADITIONALLY SLICED. THE POINT IS LOADED WITH FAT, AND THIS IS THE CUT USED TO MAKE THE FAMOUS KANSAS CITY BURNT ENDS. WHEN TRIMMING THE FLAT, YOU WANT TO LEAVE AS MUCH FAT AS POSSIBLE, BECAUSE THIS LEANER CUT NEEDS THE FAT TO KEEP FROM DRYING OUT. YOU WANT TO REMOVE A LOT OF FAT FROM THE POINT TO BE ABLE TO CREATE A DARK, CARAMELIZED BARK DIRECTLY ON THE MEAT.

THE THICKER END OF THE BRISKET CONTAINS THE POINT, AND THE THINNER END THE FLAT. IN THE CENTER, THE POINT SITS ON TOP OF THE FLAT. TO BEGIN TRIMMING, PLACE THE BRISKET FAT-SIDE DOWN TO REVEAL THE FLAT. USING A SHARP, FLEXIBLE, 8-INCH (20-CM) KNIFE (A BONING KNIFE IS AN EXCELLENT CHOICE), REMOVE ANY EXCESS FAT FROM THE FLAT. NOTE THE DIRECTION OF THE GRAIN. WHEN SLICING THE FINISHED PRODUCT YOU WILL SLICE PERPENDICULAR TO THE GRAIN, BUT THE CARAMELIZATION OF THE COOKED MEAT WILL MAKE IT DIFFICULT TO SEE THIS CLEARLY. CREATE A SLICING GUIDE BY CUTTING A 2-INCH (5-CM) PIECE OFF THE FRONT, PERPENDICULAR TO THE GRAIN. WHEN READY TO SERVE, CONTINUE SLICING EVEN, PENCIL-THIN SLICES PARALLEL TO THIS GUIDELINE.

ON ONE SIDE OF THE FLAT, NOTE A KNOB OF HARD WHITE FAT. TRIM IT AWAY COMPLETELY; THIS WILL BEGIN TO REVEAL THE POINT PORTION OF THE BRISKET. CONTINUE TO TRIM MOST OF THE FAT OFF OF THE POINT. FLIP THE BRISKET FAT-SIDE UP AND CONTINUE TO TRIM FAT FROM THE POINT. DO NOT TRIM ANY OF THE FAT OFF ABOVE THE THINNER FLAT PORTION OF THE BRISKET. NOW YOU'RE READY TO BARBECUE!

★ SPATCHCOCK CHICKEN ★ WITH TOP-SECRET BLUE RIBBON BRINE

3 whole, young chickens, about 3 pounds (1.3 kg) each (preferably hormone- and antibiotic-free, with no added water or other solutions)

Top-Secret Blue Ribbon Brine (recipe follows)

½ cup (120 ml) peanut oil

½ cup (100 g) mild chili powder

IQUE BBQ Sauce, optional (page 35)

Lemon (optional)

SPECIAL EQUIPMENT:

5-gallon (19-L) food-grade bucket

This recipe has led us to more than a few ribbons in the chicken category. Be careful when biting into this bird. We've seen many a stalwart judge overwhelmed (in a good way) by the exploding chicken juices. This is a three-day recipe, including the brine, so plan accordingly. Though it adds time, brining keeps the meat juicier and adds flavor. If you are not going to eat all of the chicken at once, after cooling, you can divide the meat into smaller portions and vacuum seal it, to freeze and use as desired.

Spatchcock the chickens. For each one, using kitchen shears, cut along each side of the backbone and remove the back (**A**). Flip the bird breast-side up and press down until the breast bone cracks (**B**).

Place the spatchcocked birds in a food-safe plastic bucket and pour brine over, so the birds are fully submerged (use plates as a weight, if necessary). Place bucket in refrigerator and brine for 12 to 24 hours.

Remove the birds from the brine and place skin-side up on a cooling rack set over a sheet pan. Dry with paper towels and refrigerate, uncovered, overnight. The exposure to the air will dry out the birds, making for crispy skin when they cook.

Prepare smoker and bring heat to 350°F (180°C). If using a kettle grill, build a two-zone fire, and use foil or a drip pan to keep chicken juices from dripping directly into the fire (see chapter 1).

A: CUT ALONG EACH SIDE OF THE
BACKBONE AND REMOVE THE BONE.

B: TURN THE BIRD OVER AND PRESS UNTIL
THE BREAST BONE CRACKS.

SPATCHCOCK CHICKEN WITH TOP-SECRET BLUE RIBBON BRINE (CONTINUED)

Rub peanut oil over the birds, then sprinkle with chili powder. There is salt in the brine, so don't use a traditional rub that has more salt in it.

Place chickens skin-side down on clean grill grate. This will help keep them moist. The skin creates a barrier, so the juices accumulate in the meat instead of dripping down into the fire. If you are using a kettle grill, place them on the cool side of the grate.

Cook for 1 hour, or until thermometer registers 160°F (71°C) in the breast and 170°F (76°C) in the thigh. Remove from cooker and let rest for 20 minutes, skin-side up.

To serve, baste the chicken with warm IQUE BBQ Sauce or a simple squeeze of lemon—or simply serve as-is, which is our preferred way to eat it.

YIELD: 10 to 12 servings

THE TRUE MEANING OF SPATCHCOCK CHICKEN

SPATCHCOCK CHICKEN IS BASICALLY THE SAME AS BUTTERFLIED CHICKEN. THOUGH SOME USE THE WORD SPATCHCOCK TO REFER TO ANY CHICKEN LESS THAN SIX WEEKS OLD, IT IS MORE WIDELY BELIEVED TO REFER TO THE METHOD OF PREPARING THE BIRD FOR COOKING. ACCORDING TO ALAN DAVIDSON, IN *THE OXFORD COMPANION TO FOOD*, ONE THEORY IS THAT THE WORD IS AN ABBREVIATION OF THE PHRASE "DISPATCH COCK," INDICATING A WAY OF GRILLING A BIRD AFTER SPLITTING IT OPEN DOWN THE BACK AND FLATTENING OUT THE TWO HALVES. WHEN THE CHICKEN IS FLATTENED LIKE THIS, IT TAKES LESS TIME TO COOK.

TOP-SECRET BLUE RIBBON BRINE

¾ gallon (2.8 L) spring water

1 quart (946 ml) low-sodium chicken broth

¾ cup (225 g) kosher salt

½ cup (120 ml) soy sauce

1 cup (150 g) packed light brown sugar

½ cup (340 g) maple syrup

¼ cup (85 g) blackstrap molasses

1 cup (235 ml) Italian salad dressing

¼ cup (60 ml) Worcestershire sauce

¼ cup (60 ml) Dijon mustard

¼ cup (60 ml) cider vinegar

1 apple, cored and cut into quarters (do not peel)

1 orange, cut into quarters

1 lemon, cut into quarters

1 onion, peeled and cut into quarters

6 cloves garlic, peeled and smashed

2 heads roasted garlic, split in half, skin on

2 chipotle peppers (canned in adobo sauce)

3 bay leaves

8 whole black peppercorns

2 tablespoons (8.6 g) dried thyme

2 tablespoons (4 g) dried sage

4 pieces candied ginger

1 cinnamon stick

2 tablespoons (15 g) chili powder

SPECIAL EQUIPMENT:

5-gallon (19-L) food-grade bucket

Bring the water, broth, salt, soy sauce, brown sugar, maple syrup, molasses, salad dressing, Worcestershire sauce, mustard, vinegar, apple, orange, lemon, onion, garlic, and chipotles to a boil in a large stockpot over medium-high heat. Remove from heat and add the bay leaves, peppercorns, thyme, sage, ginger, cinnamon, and chili powder. Using a whisk, mix ingredients well. Cover and let sit for 30 minutes.

Pour into bucket and cool to room temperature. Refrigerate overnight.

CHAPTER 3

TAILGATING AND PLAYING OUTSIDE

WE TAKE TAILGATING VERY SERIOUSLY. We take it so seriously that the e-mails start flying at least a week before every event that will find us in a parking lot with a group of our closest friends. What are we going to cook? How are we going to make it better? While most people are content with sandwiches, chips, and a cooler of beer—or, if they're really making an effort, a portable grill for sausages or brats—that's not enough for us.

We love the challenge of trying to come up with something delicious that we haven't tried before. Maybe something that nobody has tried before. And we enjoy our results immensely, as does everyone around us. Usually, at our tailgates we end up feeding not only ourselves but also the people next to us, and the people next to them, and whoever else wanders over, drawn by the smells and the gathering crowd.

The recipes in this chapter, like UnYawn's Cajun Napalm Parking Lot Gumbo and the Ultimate Steak Bomb with homemade cheese whiz, are big and excessive and perfect for crowds. But don't feel like you have to go to a football game or a concert to make them. Everything here is also well suited to any kind of outdoor gathering with a fun group of your favorite people, at your home, at theirs, or somewhere else. Some, like the Smoked Buffalo Turkey Wing Explosion, are started at home, then finished off or assembled at the gathering. And the labor in others, such as the Seven-Layer Dip of Disbelief, can easily be shared among friends.

Party planning starts now . . .

★ SEVEN-LAYER DIP OF DISBELIEF ★

This dish came about during one of our many late-night what-if sessions. We're huge fans of the seven-layer bean dip. Who isn't? And we got to thinking, "Can we make it more high-end and blow people's minds?" The beauty of this recipe is that, mind-blowing as they are together, each of the layers makes a phenomenal appetizer in its own right. This recipe will give you leftovers of the different components, which you can set out in separate bowls. Simply make more croutons, or serve with a variety of crackers.

To assemble dip: In a large foil pan, layer the first six components in the order listed. Sprinkle 1 cup (120 g) of the Blue Cheese Crumble over the Celery Root Purée. Serve with French Bread Croutons.

YIELD: 10 appetizer servings

Serving options: If you are serving this at home rather than at a tailgate, you might want to be a little more formal—but only a little. Arrange the dip in a 2-quart (1.9-L) casserole dish. For tailgating or a party at home, it might be fun to ask some of your guests to make different layers, then assemble the whole thing when you all get together.

LAYER 1:
OLD BAY SHREDDED BEEF SHORT RIBS

2 cups (475 ml) tomato juice

4 cups (946 ml) red wine

2 cups (475 ml) water

2 ancho chiles, stems and seeds removed, chopped

1 bay leaf

1 tablespoon (7.5 g) Old Bay Seasoning

2 tablespoons (30 ml) vegetable oil

2 pounds (910 g) boneless beef short ribs, trimmed of fat

Kosher salt and freshly cracked black pepper, to taste

1 cup (125 g) flour for dusting

Preheat oven to 350°F (180°C, or gas mark 4).

In a bowl, stir together the tomato juice, wine, water, chiles, bay leaf, and Old Bay Seasoning. Set aside.

In a 5- to 6-quart (4.7- to 5.7-L) Dutch oven, heat oil over medium-high heat. Season short ribs with salt and pepper, dust with flour, and sear on all sides until golden brown, about 4 to 6 minutes per side. Remove from heat and strain off oil. Carefully pour the tomato juice mixture over short ribs (liquid will splatter), cover with aluminum foil, and bake until the meat registers an internal temperature of 192°F (89°C), about 2 hours.

Let cool to room temperature, transfer meat to a cutting board, and roughly chop into small pieces. Return meat to braising liquid still in the pan and cook over medium-high heat, stirring occasionally, until the mixture has the consistency of fairly thick chili, about 1 hour. Season with salt and black pepper to taste, and cool to room temperature.

YIELD: 5½ cups (1.3 L)

LAYER 2: CRAB REMOULADE

1 pound (455 g) fresh lump crabmeat

1 tablespoon (3 g) minced chives

2 scallions, roughly chopped

¼ rib celery, roughly chopped

1 egg

1 tablespoon (4 g) chopped fresh parsley

1 tablespoon (15 ml) Dijon mustard

1 tablespoon (15 ml) ketchup

1 clove garlic, chopped

1 tablespoon (15 ml) cayenne pepper sauce, such as Frank's Red Hot Sauce

2 teaspoons (10 ml) cider vinegar

1 teaspoon (5 ml) Worcestershire sauce

¼ cup (60 ml) vegetable oil

Kosher salt and freshly cracked black pepper, to taste

Place the crabmeat in a medium bowl. Add the chives, and toss gently to combine, breaking up the crab as little as possible. Set aside.

To make the remoulade, in the bowl of a food processor, combine the scallions, celery, egg, parsley, mustard, ketchup, garlic, cayenne pepper sauce, vinegar, and Worcestershire sauce, and process until smooth. With the machine running, add the oil in a very thin stream and process until well combined.

Gradually fold enough of the remoulade into the crabmeat to coat evenly. (Reserve any leftover remoulade for another use.) Season with salt and pepper to taste.

YIELD: 3 cups (710 ml)

LAYER 3: BEEF TARTARE

2 pounds (1 kg) beef tenderloin, cleaned of all fat and sinew, finely minced

2 hard-boiled eggs, peeled and grated, and 2 raw egg yolks

½ cup (69 g) capers, rinsed and drained well

1 tablespoon (15 ml) olive oil

1 tablespoon (15 ml) Dijon mustard

Kosher salt and freshly cracked black pepper, to taste

In a bowl, combine beef, eggs, egg yolks, capers, olive oil, and mustard. Season with salt and pepper.

YIELD: 5 cups (1.2 L)

LAYER 4: SMOKED SALMON SPREAD

1 pound (455 g) cream cheese, at room temperature

½ cup (120 g) mascarpone cheese

1 pound (455 g) smoked salmon, roughly chopped

2 scallions, green parts only, cut into thin rings

Zest of 1 lemon, removed with a peeler and chopped

1 teaspoon (2 g) ground white pepper

1 cup (100 g) salmon roe

In the bowl of a stand mixer fitted with a paddle, beat cream cheese and mascarpone on medium speed until fully combined. Add salmon, scallions, zest, and white pepper, and beat on medium-high for 2 minutes, scraping down the sides of the bowl after 1 minute. Use a large spatula to fold in the salmon roe. Hey, you're more than halfway done . . .

YIELD: 4½ cups (1.1 kg)

LAYER 5: CREAMED SPINACH

2 tablespoons (28 g) butter

2 cloves garlic, minced

1 pound (455 g) fresh spinach (not baby), washed, stems removed

1 cup (235 ml) heavy cream

Kosher salt and freshly cracked black pepper, to taste

In a very large, heavy-bottomed sauté pan, melt the butter over medium heat. Add the garlic and cook for 2 minutes, stirring frequently to prevent browning. Raise heat to high and add one-third of the spinach, stirring and turning with tongs until wilted. Add the cream, then the remaining spinach in 2 batches. Continue stirring until the spinach is wilted and cream has reduced and thickened, 5 to 10 minutes. Season with salt and pepper and remove from heat. Cool to room temperature.

YIELD: 2 cups (475 ml)

LAYER 6: CELERY ROOT PURÉE

1 pound (455 g) celery root, peeled and cut into 1-inch (2.5-cm) chunks

½ pound (227 g) baking potatoes, peeled and cut into 1-inch (2.5-cm) chunks

3 cloves garlic, peeled

2 to 2½ cups (475 to 570 ml) milk

Kosher salt

Place the celery root, potatoes, and garlic in a medium sauce-pan and add cold water to cover by 1 inch (2.5 cm). Bring to a boil over high heat, then reduce the heat to medium-high and simmer for about 10 minutes, until a fork slides easily into the vegetables.

Drain the vegetables well and transfer half of them to a blender. Add 1 cup (235 ml) of the milk and purée, adding additional milk if necessary, a little at a time, to make a smooth, thick purée. Transfer to a bowl and repeat with remaining vegetables and milk. Season with salt, and cool to room temperature.

YIELD: 4 cups (950 ml)

CELERY ROOT

CELERY ROOT, WHICH ALSO GOES BY THE NAME CELERIAC, IS A FUNNY-LOOKING ROOT VEG-ETABLE. IT IS RELATED TO CELERY BUT IS GROWN FOR ITS ROOT, RATHER THAN THE LEAVES AND STEM. CELERY ROOT TASTES MILDER AND SLIGHTLY SWEETER THAN CELERY, AND IT IS EQUALLY GOOD COOKED AND RAW. WHEN SHOPPING, BE SURE TO SELECT ROOTS THAT ARE FIRM WITH LIGHT BROWN SKIN. YOU SHOULD AVOID DARK AND SOFT SPOTS, WHICH INDI-CATE ROT. CELERY ROOT CAN LAST IN THE REFRIGERATOR FOR A COUPLE OF MONTHS, BUT CHECK IT PERIODICALLY FOR SOFT SPOTS.

LAYER 7: BLUE CHEESE CRUMBLE

2 cups (230 g) crumbled saltine crackers

1 cup (120 g) crumbled blue cheese

1 cup (80 g) crumbled fried bacon

½ cup (30 g) chopped parsley

In a mixing bowl, toss all the ingredients together and set aside.

YIELD: 2 cups (240 g)

FRENCH BREAD CROUTONS

1 French baguette

Extra-virgin olive oil, for brushing

Kosher salt

Preheat oven to 400°F (200°C, or gas mark 6).

Cut the baguette on a diagonal into 5-inch-long (12.5-cm), ¼-inch-thick (6-mm) ovals. It is important that the crouton be long and stable enough to support all of the dip's goodness.

On a baking sheet, arrange the bread slices in a single layer and brush lightly with olive oil. Sprinkle lightly with salt and bake until golden brown, 6 to 8 minutes, watching closely so the croutons do not burn. Cool slightly.

YIELD: 45 croutons

★ SMOKED BUFFALO ★ TURKEY WING EXPLOSION

5 pounds (2.27 kg) turkey wings

¾ cup (75 g) Dalmatian Rub (page 139)

2 cups (475 ml) cayenne pepper sauce, such as Frank's Red Hot Sauce, divided

2 cups (4 sticks, 450 g) butter, divided

1 cup (120 g) finely crumbled blue cheese, divided

Oil for deep frying

2 cups (250 g) instant flour, such as Wondra

4 ribs celery, julienned

SPECIAL EQUIPMENT:

Marinade injector, disposable aluminum pans, deep fryer

Up here in New England, we tailgate nearly every weekend of football season, and we make it a point to never cook the old standbys like traditional hamburgers, hot dogs, or brats. We're always making something new and creative, and we readily attract friends with some of the food we pull off the grill.

Tough as we are, come December it can get a little too chilly even for us to spend the four to six hours outside that some of our dishes require. So we're big fans of a two-step process for tailgating, where a large amount of the work is done at home and finished in the parking lot. This turkey preparation is a great example of that approach.

Prepare the smoker and bring the heat to 250°F (120°C). Use a mild smoke wood, such as apple.

Using a sharp knife, cut the turkey wings into three sections—drumette, wingette, and tip. Sprinkle the drumettes and wingettes with Dalmatian Rub and smoke for 1½ to 2 hours, or until internal temperatures reach 165°F (74°C). (The wing tips can be used for turkey stock. If you are not making stock immediately, you can freeze them.) Transfer the smoked wings to a platter.

While the wings are resting, make the pepper-cheese marinade: Combine 1 cup (235 ml) cayenne pepper sauce, 1 cup (2 sticks, 225 g) butter, and ½ cup (60 g) blue cheese in a disposable aluminum roasting pan. Place on the smoker grate and heat until the butter is about three-quarters melted, about 15 minutes. Be careful not to let the butter melt completely because this may cause the sauce to break. Thoroughly whisk to blend the ingredients. Transfer to a quart-sized (946 ml) container and cool.

Fill a marinade injector with the pepper-cheese mixture and inject the smoked wings with as much marinade as they will hold. When the marinade starts spilling out of the wings, they're good to go. Place wings in a new aluminum pan, cover with foil, and refrigerate for 2 hours or overnight.

At your tailgate, set up a deep fryer, and bring the oil temperature to 375°F (190°C). On a grill or portable camp stove, warm the remaining 1 cup (235 ml) cayenne pepper sauce and 1 cup (2 sticks, 225 g) butter.

Dredge the wings in instant flour and deep-fry in batches for 3 to 5 minutes each. In a large mixing bowl, toss the fried wings with the warm cayenne/butter mixture. Sprinkle the remaining ½ cup (60 g) blue cheese and the celery over the wings and serve—with extra napkins.

YIELD: 8 servings (or enough for 3 drunk guys)

★ UNYAWN'S CAJUN NAPALM ★ PARKING LOT GUMBO

8 whole chickens, about 4 pounds (1.8 kg) each

1 cup (200 g) granulated garlic

½ cup (50 g) ground black pepper

4 gallons (15 L) water

5 pounds (2.27 kg) chicken wings

8 large onions, 2 sliced and 6 chopped

1 bunch parsley, stems removed and reserved, tips chopped

2 cups (475 ml) peanut oil

2 cups (250 g) all-purpose flour

3 heads garlic, minced

2 whole bunches celery, chopped

4 green bell peppers, seeds removed, chopped

5 pounds (2.27 kg) smoked andouille sausage, sliced

Kosher salt, black pepper, and cayenne pepper, to taste

4 bunches scallions, chopped

½ cup (120 ml) hot pepper sauce, such as Tabasco

Cooked white rice, for serving

SPECIAL EQUIPMENT:

10-gallon (37.8-L) gumbo pot, food-handling gloves, propane burner (if you're not near your stove), food-safe 5-gallon (19-L) bucket

With five hundred barbecue enthusiasts crammed into a parking lot for a long weekend, the party is lively, to say the least. Over the years we've found a direct correlation between how well we score at the American Royal competition in Kansas City and the amount of time we spend at the Jamaican national team's open bar on Friday night. Our cooking site every year is right next to the Motley Que Crew, whose team member Ron Walker, widely known as only "UnYawn," cooks up a mean pot of smoked chicken gumbo. One late night after a few beers, he shared the recipe with us. If you're not cooking for a whole parking lot full of people, the recipe can be halved. It also freezes well.

Prepare smoker and bring heat to 250°F (120°C).

Cut the whole chickens in half and season liberally with granulated garlic and black pepper. Smoke until breast reaches internal temperature of 160°F (71°C), about 2 hours. Remove the chickens from the cooker and let cool a bit. With gloved hands, pull meat from the bones, reserving bones and skin. Refrigerate the meat.

In the gumbo pot, bring the reserved smoked chicken bones and skin, water, chicken wings, and the 2 sliced onions to a boil over high heat. Reduce heat and add parsley stems. Simmer for 2 hours, then strain into a food-safe bucket. The chicken stock can be made in advance and refrigerated or frozen.

Heat oil in a deep saucepan over medium heat, and sift in flour to make a roux, stirring constantly. The roux may bubble and pop small hot bits onto your arm (hence the name "Cajun Napalm"). Reduce heat to low and stir with a flat-bottomed wooden spatula until the roux is a dark chocolate color, being very careful not to burn it. Add the 6 chopped onions, minced garlic, celery, and bell pepper, and sauté until vegetables are soft. Add a little reserved smoked chicken stock to avoid sticking, and continue to cook for another 20 minutes, stirring constantly. Stir in smoked andouille and remaining stock, and simmer for about 1 hour more. Add salt, black pepper, and cayenne to taste. When the stock is thick and dark brown, add the refrigerated chicken meat and continue cooking at a low simmer until heated through. Add the scallions, hot pepper sauce, and chopped parsley tips. Check for seasoning and add cayenne as desired.

To serve, mound white rice in bowls, and ladle gumbo over.

YIELD: 25 servings

★ MUFFIN TIN SMOKIN' SLIDERS ★
WITH 647 SECRET SAUCE

FOR CARAMELIZED ONIONS:

2 tablespoons (30 ml) olive oil

3 large sweet onions, sliced

1 teaspoon (6 g) salt

1 tablespoon (15 ml) water

FOR SEASONED SALT:

¾ cup (225 g) kosher salt

2 tablespoons (26 g) sugar

2 tablespoons (14 g) paprika

1 tablespoon (6.5 g) celery salt

1 tablespoon (9 g) garlic powder

1 tablespoon (6.9 g) onion powder

1 teaspoon (2.2 g) ground turmeric

½ teaspoon (0.9 g) dried oregano

½ teaspoon (2.15 g) ground thyme

⅛ teaspoon (0.3 g) ground cinnamon

FOR BURGERS:

2½ pounds (1.14 kg) freshly ground chuck, 80% lean

9 slices deli-style American cheese, quartered

Buttermilk Slider Rolls (recipe follows)

647 Secret Sauce (recipe follows)

One 16-ounce (455-g) jar dill pickle chips

SPECIAL EQUIPMENT:

Muffin tins with 4-ounce (120 ml) cups (or disposable aluminum muffin tins), enough for 18 sliders

Nothing is more all-American than burgers on the grill. Sliders are burgers' new-century party incarnation. Cooking them over fire in muffin tins is so much easier than flipping them all individually, and lining the tins with caramelized onions imparts the vegetables' sweet, rich flavor to the meat while they cook. Sheer genius, if we do say so ourselves. We like to serve them on our own buttermilk rolls because, really, what is better than homemade bread in any form? (You can buy rolls, but they won't be as good.) Pass these babies with a few other appetizers, and you've got yourself a party.

Prepare your smoker or kettle grill and bring temperature to 300°F (150°C).

To caramelize the onions: Heat the olive oil in a large, non-stick sauté pan over medium-high heat. Add the onions and salt and cook, stirring often, until onions soften and just start to brown. Reduce heat to medium-low and cook, stirring occasionally, until onions collapse completely and turn a rich, jammy brown, about 30 minutes. When onions are nearly done, add the water and stir, scraping the browned bits on the bottom of the pan into the onions. Set aside to cool.

To make the seasoned salt: In a bowl, mix all ingredients together, then grind in a spice grinder.

To make the burgers: Divide the ground beef into 18 golf ball–sized rounds (about 2½ ounces, or 55 g each). Spread about ¼ cup (72 g) seasoned salt on a plate and roll the balls lightly in the seasoned salt to coat.

Spread 1 tablespoon (5.5 g) of caramelized onions in the bottom of each muffin cup (A). Place 1 meatball on top of the onion in each cup and press down with your fingers to form into an even burger (B).

A: PLACE CARAMELIZED ONIONS IN BOTTOM OF EACH MUFFIN PAN

B: PRESS MEAT DOWN WITH YOUR FINGERS TO FORM EVEN BURGERS.

C: OVERLAP SLICES OF CHEESE ON EACH BURGER.

Put the muffin tins on the grill grate, close the lid, and cook for 30 minutes. Remove the muffin tins, overlap 2 quarter-slices of American cheese on each burger, and tent the muffin tins with foil (**c**).

If your slider rolls are not fresh from the oven, wrap in foil and place on the smoker for 5 minutes, or microwave for 20 seconds. You want the slider rolls to be soft and squishy inside.

To serve, use tongs to transfer the burgers from the tins to the slider rolls. Then, with the tongs, pick up some of the remaining onions and place on top of the burger. Garnish with a generous schmear of 647 Secret Sauce and pickle chips.

YIELD: 18 sliders

647 SECRET SAUCE

¼ **cup (60 g) mayonnaise**

¼ **cup (35 g) finely chopped dill pickles, drained well**

2 **tablespoons (30 ml) Dijon or spicy brown mustard**

2 **tablespoons (30 ml) ketchup**

½ **teaspoon (2 g) sugar, or more to taste**

Freshly cracked black pepper, to taste

This sauce, a favorite on the burgers at Andy's restaurant, Tremont 647, is great to have on hand any time you're cooking with fire. This recipe can be doubled easily.

In a bowl, mix all ingredients together. Cover and chill. Before serving, taste to correct seasoning with sugar and pepper.

The sauce will keep, covered tightly and refrigerated, for up to 2 months.

YIELD: ¾ cup (175 g)

BUTTERMILK SLIDER ROLLS

6 tablespoons (¾ stick, 85 g) butter

⅓ cup (67 g) sugar

1¼ cups (295 ml) buttermilk

4 cups (500 g) flour

1 tablespoon (18 g) kosher salt

1 packet (2¼ teaspoons, 9 g) active dry yeast, dissolved in ½ cup (120 ml) warm water

SPECIAL EQUIPMENT:

Muffin tins with 4-ounce (120-ml) cups

These delicious rolls are soft and pillowy inside, with a nice crunchy crust. In addition to going perfectly with the sliders, they are heavenly wrapped around a dollop (or two) of Bacon Jam (page 108).

In a small saucepan over medium heat, stir the butter and sugar until the butter melts. Add the buttermilk and blend well. In the bowl of a stand mixer, blend flour, salt, buttermilk mixture, and yeast with a large rubber spatula until moistened. Using the dough hook, beat the dough at lowest speed until it starts to pull away from the sides of the bowl. Increase speed to medium and beat until dough is smooth, about 5 minutes.

Place dough in a lightly oiled mixing bowl, cover with lightly oiled plastic wrap and a towel, and let rise in a warm place for 1 hour, until doubled in size.

Preheat oven to 350°F (180°C, or gas mark 4).

Divide dough evenly among 18 greased muffin cups. Cover loosely with oiled or sprayed plastic wrap and let rise in a warm place for 30 minutes. Remove the plastic wrap and bake until tops are puffed and golden, 15 to 20 minutes.

YIELD: 18 rolls

★ WOOD-GRILLED PARTY PANINI ★

FOR VEGETABLES:

¼ cup (60 ml) each balsamic and red wine vinegar

2 cups (475 ml) extra-virgin olive oil

1 teaspoon (1.2 g) crushed red pepper flakes

2 teaspoons (3.6 g) dried oregano

2 shallots, minced

½ cup (30 g) chopped Italian flat-leaf parsley

Kosher salt and freshly cracked black pepper

6 red onions, peeled and sliced ⅛ inch (3 mm) thick

10 plum tomatoes, cored and sliced ¼ inch (6 mm) thick

1 fennel bulb, tops and core removed, sliced paper-thin (preferably using a mandolin)

FOR SANDWICHES:

2 loaves Italian-style bread, about 1½ feet (45 cm) long

2 pounds (1 kg) provolone, thinly sliced

2 pounds (1 kg) hot capicola, thinly sliced

2 pounds (1 kg) Mortadella, thinly sliced

2 pounds (1 kg) Genoa salami, thinly sliced

30 pepperoncini, stems removed and sliced ¼ inch (6 mm) thick

6 roasted red peppers, peeled, seeded, cored, and cut into large pieces

10 leaves romaine lettuce, washed and patted dry

¼ cup (60 ml) olive oil for brushing bread

SPECIAL EQUIPMENT:

6 to 8 bricks, wrapped in foil

We have a sizable group of friends who go to a lot of football games together, and over the years our tailgates have become something of a competition. We take turns planning the meal, and not only do we try to one-up each other for the most outrageously delicious creations, but we also love watching the faces of people around us when they see the feast we're laying out. For one very important game, a couple of us decided to make the biggest panini we could, improvising the Italian sandwich press on our grill. The most important step here is marinating the vegetables so the high notes and richness of the vinaigrette stay within the sandwich. Of course, you need to flip carefully, too, so the meat itself stays in the bread.

To make the vegetables: In a medium mixing bowl, combine the balsamic and red wine vinegars, olive oil, red pepper flakes, dried oregano, shallots, and parsley, and liberally season with salt and pepper (you want it to be a little on the salty/peppery side). Add the onions, tomatoes, and fennel and toss to coat the vegetables with the vinaigrette. Let sit for 10 minutes, toss again, and let sit for 10 minutes more.

To make the sandwiches: Slice the loaves in half lengthwise, then cut in half and lay the bottoms cut-side up on the counter or a large jelly-roll pan. Build the panini by evenly layering the cheese and meats on top of the bread (A). Spread the pepperoncini and roasted peppers evenly on top.

Strain the marinating vegetables and evenly spread over the panini. Reserve the marinade/vinaigrette to use for dipping when sandwiches are done. Place the romaine leaves over the vegetables and top each sandwich with the other piece of bread.

A: MEATS, CHEESES, AND VEGETABLES LAYERED ON BREAD.

B: BRICKS AND GRILL AS PANINI PRESS.

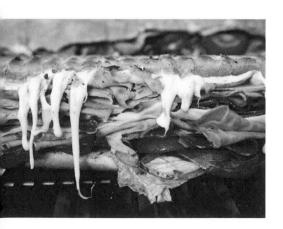

C: ALMOST READY . . .

WOOD-GRILLED PARTY PANINI (CONTINUED)

Fill a chimney half full with hardwood lump charcoal and two pieces of newspaper, and light. When flames are just starting to peek through the top of the charcoal, transfer coals to a kettle grill. When they have all reached maximum heat (you should only be able to hold your hand over the coals for 5 seconds), spread coals out in a single layer. Let the fire die down before you start grilling, so you don't burn the bread. When you can hold your hand over the fire for 15 to 20 seconds, it's time to start.

Place the panini on a clean grill rack over the coals. Place a large sheet pan on top of the sandwiches, and place the bricks on top of the pan (B). Cook for 5 minutes. Carefully remove the bricks (they may be warm/hot). Using spatulas and the help of at least one friend, very carefully turn the panini over. Replace the sheet pan and bricks and cook for 5 minutes more.

Again using your spatula and your friend(s), remove the panini and place on a large cutting board (C). Using a serrated knife, cut along a diagonal into 2- to 3-inch (5- to 7.5-cm) pieces. Serve hot, either drizzled with reserved vinaigrette or using the vinaigrette as a dipping sauce.

YIELD: 10 to 15 servings

★ STEAK AND CHEESE HOT POPPERS ★

One 8-ounce (225-g) rib-eye steak

Kosher salt and freshly cracked black pepper, to taste

1 tablespoon (15 ml) vegetable oil

1 small yellow onion, sliced

1 head roasted garlic, cloves processed into a smooth paste

1½ cups (345 g) cream cheese, softened

½ cup (58 g) shredded extra-sharp cheddar cheese

12 whole jalapeño peppers, halved lengthwise, seeds and ribs removed (wear gloves)

12 slices bacon, cut in half, at room temperature

¼ cup (30 g) IQUE Dry Rub (page 32)

It's pretty hard to go wrong with ingredients like bacon, steak, garlic, cheese, and jalapeño peppers. The poppers are a great tailgate item that should be fully prepped at home, then cooked for two hours at your party. Whether you're serving them at home or in a parking lot, we recommend doubling the recipe, as we have never had leftovers of this addictive snack. If you want to make the poppers truly atomic, try adding a sliver of habanero pepper to the inside of each one.

Heat a cast-iron pan over medium-high heat until it is quite hot. Season the steak with salt and pepper and sear for 3 to 4 minutes on each side until there is a caramelized crust and the meat has an internal temperature of 135°F (57.2°C). Cook over medium heat until medium-rare. Transfer steak to a cutting board and let rest for 20 minutes. Add oil to the pan and sauté the onion for 5 to 7 minutes, until soft.

In a large bowl, combine the onion and garlic paste. Slice the rib eye into thin strips and stir into the onion-garlic mixture.

In another bowl, stir the cream cheese and cheddar cheese together.

Spoon 1 tablespoon (15 g) cream cheese mixture into each pepper half. Top with about 1 tablespoon (15 g) steak mixture. Wrap half a slice of bacon around each half and secure with a toothpick. Refrigerate the poppers for at least 1 hour, or overnight.

Prepare smoker and bring temperature to 250°F (120°C). Sprinkle dry rub on each popper, and smoke for 2 hours, or until the bacon is crisp. Serve immediately.

YIELD: 24 poppers

★ TNTUBE STEAK FROM HELL ★

One 5-pound (2.27-kg) bologna chub

¾ cup (175 ml) yellow mustard

¾ cup (75 g) IQUE Dry Rub (page 32)

1 cup (235 ml) canned nacho cheese sauce

1 quart (946 ml) Chili from Hell (recipe follows)

1 medium onion, minced

1 cup (115 g) crumbled corn chips

1 cup (80 g) minced cooked bacon

½ cup (65 g) Habanero Mash (recipe follows)

One of the advantages of being northern guys in the barbecue world is that we didn't come into it bound by years of tradition. We don't really have a barbecue culture where we come from, so for us, anything goes. If we want to mix barbecued bologna (a staple in Memphis) with Texas chili (yeah, that's right, no beans!) and top it with Habanero Mash instead of coleslaw, nobody's going to stop us. We just go by what tastes good and start our own traditions.

Prepare smoker and bring temperature to 250°F (120°C). Use a mild smoke wood, such as apple.

Place bologna on a cutting board. Score a 1-inch (2.5-cm) -deep slit around the circumference of the chub every 3 inches (7.5 cm) along its length. Cover bologna with mustard and sprinkle dry rub all over.

Smoke bologna for 4 hours. Remove and let meat rest for 30 minutes.

Just before serving, warm the nacho cheese in a saucepan over low heat. Watch it closely, making sure it does not bubble.

Slice the bologna into ¾-inch (1.7-cm) slabs. Place one slab on a plate and top with Chili from Hell, nacho cheese sauce, onion, corn chips, and bacon. Add a dollop of Habanero Mash. Eat immediately, ideally while standing in a stadium parking lot with a cold beer, getting ready to go in to watch a football game.

YIELD: 12 to 14 servings

CHILI FROM HELL

2 pounds (905 g) ground beef, 85% lean

6 tablespoons (45 g) high-quality chili powder*

2 tablespoons (18 g) garlic powder

One 7-ounce (205 ml) can chipotle peppers in adobo sauce

One 14-ounce (425 ml) can low-sodium beef broth

We really enjoy beating Texans at barbecue contests. But one thing we listen to them on is the right way to make chili. Namely, *no beans or tomatoes allowed*. Here is a version that will please your chile-head friends and bring heat neophytes to their knees. This chili leans toward the dry side; the consistency is akin to Sloppy Joes or taco meat. Eat it on its own, or in a TNTube Steak from Hell.

In a large cast-iron Dutch oven over medium-high heat, brown the ground beef and drain off all but 2 tablespoons (30 ml) of the grease. Add the chili powder and garlic powder, mixing to completely coat the meat. Adjust the heat so the chili cooks gently, without scorching, for 15 minutes (mixture will look dry).

While the meat is cooking, purée the chipotles in a blender. Add the chipotles and beef broth to the meat and mix well. Simmer gently for 1 hour, stirring often to prevent scorching.

YIELD: 5 cups (1.18 L)

* We recommend using fresh chili powder, such as Gebhardt's, which has superior flavor. It can be difficult to find at traditional grocery stores, but you can find sources online. Other options are the custom chili blends available from Pendery's (see Resources, page 218) or any good spice shop in your neighborhood.

HABANERO MASH

1 pound (455 g) carrots (about 4 large), peeled and cut into 3-inch (7.5-cm) chunks

1 medium yellow onion, roughly chopped

6 habanero peppers, stemmed

4 cloves garlic, peeled

½ cup (120 ml) white vinegar

½ cup (120 ml) water, as needed

Kosher salt and freshly cracked black pepper, to taste

With six habanero peppers, this mash would register pretty high on the Scoville scale. But you can take it (or you can cut back on the peppers a little bit). This is delicious with the TNTube Steak from Hell, and if you're a chile-head, we also recommend it stirred into UnYawn's Cajun Napalm Parking Lot Gumbo (page 66).

Place a steamer rack in the bottom of a large saucepan. Add just enough water to touch the bottom of the rack; place carrots on rack. Cover pan and steam over medium-high heat until carrots are just tender, 6 to 7 minutes.

Place the steamed carrots, onion, habaneros, garlic, and vinegar into a blender and purée until smooth. If mixture is too thick, add water as needed. Season the mash with salt and pepper. Mash will keep, refrigerated in an airtight container, for up to 1 month.

YIELD: 3 cups (750 ml)

★ WHOLE SMOKE-ROASTED ★ STRIPED BASS AND ROCKET PESTO

1 whole striped bass or salmon, around 20 to 30 pounds (9 to 13.7 kg), scaled

2 cups (475 ml) olive oil

5 cloves garlic, roughly chopped

5 cups (300 g) fresh Italian parsley leaves, plus 1 whole bunch fresh Italian parsley

8 sprigs rosemary, needles removed and stems discarded

1 cup (235 ml) fresh lemon juice

¼ cup (75 g) kosher salt

2 tablespoons (12 g) ground black pepper

2 cups (80 g) loosely packed basil leaves

10 tarragon sprigs

12 thyme sprigs

Rocket Pesto (recipe follows)

Cheesy Grilled Corn (recipe follows)

Chris Schlesinger, chef-owner of East Coast Grill in Cambridge, Massachusetts, is largely responsible for getting us into barbecue. His Fourth of July parties in Westport, Massachusetts, may be right up there with his reputation as a chef, restaurateur, and cookbook author. Every year on the holiday, friends of Chef Schlesinger bring 30- to 50-pound (13.7- to 22.8-kg) whole bass that they've just caught, and he usually asks us to cook them.

There is nothing better than smoky whole fish just off the fire. Like bone-in meat, fish retains its moisture best when you cook it whole. We came up with this recipe the first year we were asked to cook one, and it was so good, it's been a keeper. We grilled sweet corn with it, which is a perfect complement to the rich, smoky fish.

Because we're dealing with significant bulk, and fish sizes are so variable, it's hard to provide a definitive cook time. Our friend Wade Wiestling, vice president of culinary development at the Oceanaire Seafood Room, gave us a great guideline: cook 5 minutes per inch (2.5 cm) at the fish's largest circumference, at 400°F (200°C). This recipe serves a lot of people, so plan on a big party.

Make sure the fish has had all its scales removed, and that the inside cavity is clean. If there are any scales left, remove them using the back of a knife to scrape the skin from tail to head. Pat the skin dry with a towel.

Prepare smoker and bring heat to 400°F (200°C). We recommend oak or hickory as the smoke wood.

A: STUFF THE FISH CAVITY WITH
ASSORTED HERBS.

B: SMOKE UNTIL THE FISH'S INTERNAL
TEMPERATURE REACHES 140°F (60°C).

C: ROLL CORN ON GRATE TO TOAST ALL
SIDES AND KEEP IT FROM BURNING.

WHOLE SMOKE-ROASTED STRIPED BASS AND ROCKET PESTO (CONTINUED)

In a blender, purée the olive oil, garlic, 5 cups (300 g) parsley leaves, rosemary, lemon juice, salt, and pepper until smooth. Coat the fish with the herb mixture inside and out. Stuff the cavity with the basil, tarragon, thyme, and remaining 1 bunch parsley (A).

Transfer fish to a large foil-lined baking sheet, and smoke for 5 minutes for every inch (2.5 cm) the fish measures at its largest circumference, or until the fish's internal temperature reaches 140°F (60°C)(B).

To serve, gently transfer roasted fish to a large platter or cutting board and drizzle with Rocket Pesto. Serve with Cheesy Grilled Corn.

YIELD: 20 to 30 servings

ROCKET PESTO

1½ cups (220 g) pistachios, shells removed, toasted

3 cloves garlic, chopped

½ cup (50 g) grated Parmigiano-Reggiano

1 pound (455 g) arugula (also known as rocket)

2 cups (475 ml) olive oil

Kosher salt and freshly cracked black pepper, to taste

Pesto is traditionally made with basil, garlic, parmesan or pecorino cheese, pine nuts, and olive oil, but we thought we'd shake things up a bit by replacing the basil with arugula and substituting pistachios for pine nuts.

In a food processor, purée the pistachios, garlic, and cheese. Add arugula and pulse to combine. With the motor running, slowly drizzle in the olive oil. Season with salt and pepper.

YIELD: 4 cups (946 ml)

CHEESY GRILLED CORN

FOR AIOLI:

2 egg yolks

2 cloves garlic, chopped

2 tablespoons (30 ml) fresh lemon juice

2 cups (475 ml) vegetable oil

Kosher salt and freshly cracked black pepper, to taste

FOR CORN:

20 ears corn, shucked, snapped in half, and blanched for 30 seconds

4 cups (480 g) crumbled queso fresco (if you can't find queso fresco, feta works as well)

½ cup (64 g) chili powder

10 limes, cut into 6 wedges each

Grilled corn with cotija cheese (a hard, dry cheese named for the town in Mexico from whence it originates), mayonnaise, and a dusting of chili powder is popular street food in Mexico. One bite and it's easy to see why. Here's our version.

To make the aioli: In the bowl of a food processor, purée the egg yolks, garlic, and lemon juice. With the motor running, slowly drizzle in oil to combine. Season with salt and pepper. Transfer to a bowl and reserve.

To make the corn: Prepare grill. When fire is medium-hot (you should not be able to hold your hand over the coals for more than 10 seconds), grill corn for about 5 minutes, rolling it to toast all sides and keep it from burning (c). Remove from grill and slather with aioli, then sprinkle with queso fresco and chili powder. Serve with lime wedges.

YIELD: 20 servings

★ ULTIMATE STEAK BOMB ★

FOR STEAK:

½ cup (150 g) kosher salt

2 tablespoons (36 g) garlic salt

3 tablespoons (21 g) onion powder

3 tablespoons (9 g) dried dill

2 tablespoons (10 g) coriander seeds, toasted and coarsely ground

¼ cup (25 g) coarsely ground black pepper

¼ cup (25 g) paprika

1 tablespoon (5.3 g) cayenne pepper

1 whole rib eye, about 8 to 9 pounds (3.63 to 4.09 kg), most of the fat trimmed off

5 pounds (2.27 kg) portobello mushroom caps

Kosher salt and freshly cracked black pepper, to taste

FOR PICKLED PEPPERS:

4 green bell peppers, cored and julienned

4 red bell peppers, cored and julienned

½ cup (50 g) fennel seeds

1 tablespoon (3.6 g) crushed red pepper flakes

1 cup (235 ml) white vinegar

¼ cup (60 ml) water

½ cup (100 g) sugar

½ tablespoon (9 g) salt

2 teaspoons (9 g) celery salt

Our barbecue team always makes a big, easy meal the night before a competition begins, and this is one of our favorites. Different members use different condiments, but the foundation doesn't change much. The rub is based on McCormick's Montreal Steak Seasoning. We like to use rib eye, which costs a little more than other cuts, but we think is totally worth it. (You can substitute shaved steak if you like.) If you're not competing the next day, this is also a great party dish; it's definitely for a large group. If you use rib eye, you might want to get your hands on a meat slicer.

To make the steak: In a small bowl, combine the salt, garlic salt, onion powder, dill, coriander, pepper, paprika, and cayenne pepper, then liberally rub and press all over the rib eye.

Prepare smoker and bring heat to 300°F (150°C). We recommend oak or hickory as the smoke wood.

Smoke the steak for 45 minutes to 1 hour, or until internal temperature registers 110°F (43°C). It will still be very rare. Wearing heatproof gloves, remove meat from smoker. Rest on a rack set into a sheet pan for 20 minutes, then refrigerate for at least 3 hours, or until the meat registers an internal temperature below 41°F (5°C).

While the meat is resting, smoke the mushrooms for 15 minutes, until tender. Slice thinly, season with salt and pepper, and set aside.

Once the rib eye has cooled completely, transfer to a cutting board and slice as thinly as possible, basically "shaving" it. If you have access to a meat slicer, this will give you the most traditional "shaved steak" possible.

FOR CARAMELIZED ONIONS AND GARLIC:

3 tablespoons (45 ml) olive oil

4 large yellow onions, julienned

4 cloves garlic, minced

Kosher salt and freshly cracked black pepper, to taste

FOR SANDWICHES:

¼ cup (60 ml) vegetable oil

Kosher salt and freshly cracked black pepper, to taste

2 loaves Italian-style bread, cut in half lengthwise

Cheese Dizzle (recipe follows)

SPECIAL EQUIPMENT:

Heatproof gloves, 6-inch (15-cm) frilled toothpicks or skewers

To make the pickled peppers: Place all ingredients in a small saucepan over high heat and bring to a boil, stirring occasionally. Lower heat and simmer for 10 minutes. Remove from heat and strain, reserving pickled peppers.

To make the caramelized onions and garlic: In a heavy-bottomed sauté pan, heat the oil over medium-high heat. Add the onions and cook, stirring occasionally, until softened, about 5 minutes. Turn heat to low and add the garlic. Cook, stirring occasionally, until the onions are lightly caramelized, about 15 minutes. Season with salt and pepper. Keep warm or at room temperature until ready to serve.

To assemble this monstrosity: Prepare a kettle grill. When coals reach maximum heat (you can't hold your hand over them for more than 5 seconds), spread them evenly over the bottom of grill. (If you only have a smoker, which you used to cook the steak in the first step, you can follow the manufacturer's instructions to use it for high-heat grilling, or this step can be done on a stove top.)

Place a 12- to 16-inch (30- to 40-cm) cast-iron pan on the grill. Once it's very hot, add 2 tablespoons (30 ml) oil, then half of the sliced meat, and cook meat to desired doneness; we like to leave a bit of pink. Transfer to a plate. Repeat with the remaining oil and meat. Season with salt and pepper.

Place bread cut-side down on grill rack and toast for about 30 seconds, until it turns light brown. (If you're cooking the meat inside, "toast" bread in the broiler.)

Place loaf bottoms cut-side up on the counter, a large cutting board, or a platter. Evenly layer the meat on the bread. Top with the mushrooms, pickled peppers, and caramelized onions and garlic, then drizzle with Cheese Dizzle. Place loaf tops on the sandwiches, insert toothpicks roughly 4 inches (10 cm) apart, cut into sandwiches, and serve on a platter.

YIELD: 15 to 20 servings

CHEESE DIZZLE

2 cans (5 ounces, or 150 ml, each) evaporated milk

1 pound (455 g) yellow cheddar cheese, grated

1 pound (455 g) white American cheese (or Fontina if you want to be fancy), grated or sliced

2 tablespoons (30 ml) Dijon mustard

2 tablespoons (30 ml) cider vinegar

We loved processed cheese sauce like Cheese Whiz when we were kids, but we've grown up and our taste is more sophisticated. We make our own now, and it's better than anything we ever squirted out of a can.

In a 2-quart (1.9-L) heavy-bottomed saucepan over medium-low heat, bring the evaporated milk to a simmer, and continue cooking for 5 minutes. Add remaining ingredients, stirring constantly, until well combined. Keep warm and use immediately, or refrigerate until ready to use. The dizzle can be reheated in the microwave.

YIELD: 1 quart (946 ml)

★ ATOMIC BUFFALO QUAIL ★

FOR MARINADE:

1 cup (235 ml) buttermilk

1 tablespoon (15 ml) cayenne pepper sauce, such as Frank's Red Hot Sauce

1 teaspoon (6 g) salt

FOR QUAIL:

4 quail, semi-boneless, cut in half

Vegetable oil, for frying (if you don't have a deep fryer, you'll need about 1 inch [2.5 cm] of oil)

1 jalapeño pepper, seeded, cored, and cut thin

4 slices applewood-smoked bacon

FOR SAUCE:

2 slices applewood-smoked bacon, minced

1 tablespoon (15 ml) olive oil

1 clove garlic, minced

1 tablespoon (2.5 g) minced fresh sage

½ cup (120 ml) cayenne pepper sauce

2 tablespoons (28 g) unsalted butter

1 tablespoon (8 g) grated fresh horseradish

FOR GARNISH:

4 ribs celery, cut into sticks

½ cup (30 g) finely chopped fresh parsley

¼ cup (30 g) crumbled Maytag blue cheese

SPECIAL EQUIPMENT:

8 toothpicks or skewers

One year at Memphis in May, one of the biggest barbecue competitions in the world, IQUE worked with the folks from Frank's Red Hot Sauce. Andy was inspired to develop this dish to serve in his restaurant—a sort of upscale version of traditional Buffalo wings. It is a great way to impress your guests, and can be doubled easily.

To make the marinade: In a large bowl, stir together the buttermilk, cayenne pepper sauce, and salt.

To make the quail: Place quail pieces in the bowl with the marinade, tossing to make sure they are completely coated. Cover and refrigerate for 2 hours. Remove pieces and pat dry.

In a deep fryer, preheat oil to 350°F (180°C; if you do not have a deep fryer, you can use a deep sauté pan). Preheat oven to 350°F (180°C, or gas mark 4).

Divide the jalapeño slices evenly and place in the quail cavities. Wrap the bacon slices around the quail, threading the toothpicks or skewers through the bacon, into the quail, and back out through the bacon to secure it. Deep-fry the quail for 3 to 4 minutes, until they are golden brown. Remove from oil and pat dry with paper towels. Remove toothpicks and transfer quail to a 9-inch (23-cm) square baking pan. Set aside.

To make the sauce: In a small, heavy-bottomed saucepan over medium-high heat, cook the bacon in oil until golden brown. Add the garlic and cook for 30 seconds. Reduce heat to medium-low and stir in the sage, cayenne pepper sauce, butter, and horseradish. Simmer for 5 minutes, stirring occasionally.

Spoon sauce over quail and bake for 10 minutes.

Remove quail from baking dish and transfer to a serving platter. Garnish with celery sticks, parsley, and blue cheese.

YIELD: 4 appetizer servings

★ TURKEY SKIN CHIPS ★
WITH BLUE CHEESE VINAIGRETTE

2 pounds (1 kg) turkey skin

2 tablespoons (36 g) salt, or to taste

¼ cup (½ stick, or 55 g) butter

¼ cup (60 ml) your favorite hot sauce

Blue Cheese Vinaigrette (recipe follows)

When we're competing down South, there's not much we like to munch on more than pork rinds. This is our northern twist. They're sweet, spicy, and crunchy, with nice turkey flavor. The recipe can be multiplied easily.

Preheat oven to 350°F (180°C, or gas mark 4).

Line a baking sheet with parchment paper.

Using the back of a knife, gently scrape the inside of the turkey skin to remove excess fat, keeping the skin as intact as possible. Arrange skins, as flat as possible, on the baking sheet; do not let them overlap. Sprinkle evenly with salt. Place another sheet of parchment on the skins, and lay another baking sheet on top of that to keep skins pressed flat. Bake for 40 to 45 minutes, or until skins are crisp, rotating the trays halfway through baking.

While skins are baking, in a small saucepan over medium heat, warm butter with hot sauce until butter is melted. Cool to room temperature, then transfer to a mister.

To serve, break skins into smaller, potato chip–sized pieces and mist with butter/hot sauce mixture. Serve in a large bowl, with Blue Cheese Vinaigrette on the side.

YIELD: 4 to 8 servings

BLUE CHEESE VINAIGRETTE

¼ cup (60 ml) champagne vinegar

¼ cup (30 g) crumbled blue cheese

¾ cup (175 ml) olive oil

¼ cup (15 g) roughly chopped
Italian parsley leaves

2 tablespoons (4.8 g) thyme leaves

Salt and freshly cracked black pepper, to taste

This is a recipe from Andy's first book, which he co-authored with food writer Joe Yonan. It's crisp and light, yet has a viscosity that is perfect with the fried skins.

Combine all the ingredients in a food processor or blender and purée. Transfer to a bowl and refrigerate. Stir well immediately before use.

YIELD: 1¼ cups (285 ml)

★ CHAPTER 4 ★

TWISTED TRADITIONALS

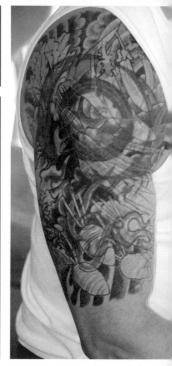

OUR MOMS ARE BOTH GREAT COOKS, but when we were growing up, other than on special occasions, our diets were no more exotic than those of our friends. As a result, we have the same nostalgic attachment most people do to standards like macaroni and cheese, meatloaf, and baked beans. These are some of our guilty pleasures. We still love them and still make them. But, being who we are, we can't just make them the way we ate them when we were kids. We need to manipulate even the most traditional dishes, to see where we can take them—usually out-of-doors and over an open fire.

In some ways, it's just an adult version of playing with our food, something we would not have dared to do when we were young—at least not at the dinner table. Now even our mothers approve of what we're doing, which is great because playing with, or riffing on, the classics got us to the $100 Meatloaf, which unites beef, veal, and foie gras in a loaf that bears only the most fleeting resemblance to anything mama ever made. It got us to Surf 'n Turf Lobster Chowder, a delectable twist on a grand New England tradition, in which native lobster amicably yields center stage to a rich and crunchy piece of smoke-braised pork belly. And on a sweet note, it got us to our Minted Molten S'Mores Cake, a sophisticated play on every kid's favorite campfire dessert.

★ THE $100 MEATLOAF ★

FOR MEATLOAF:

2 ounces (60 g) dried porcini mushrooms

2 cups (475 ml) hot water

1 pound (455 g) beef chuck, cut into ½-inch (1.3-cm) cubes

½ pound (227.5 g) veal chuck, cut into ½-inch (1.3-cm) cubes

3 tablespoons (45 ml) good-quality olive oil, divided

1 medium yellow onion, diced

1 tablespoon (10 g) garlic, minced

½ teaspoon (0.4 g) minced fresh rosemary

1 tablespoon (16 g) tomato paste

1 cup (115 g) panko or bread crumbs

2 eggs, beaten

¾ cup (180 ml) ketchup, divided

2 tablespoons (30 ml) Worcestershire sauce

¼ cup (60 ml) whole milk

Kosher salt and freshly cracked black pepper, to taste

5-ounce (150 g) piece foie gras, about 4 to 5 inches (10 to 13 cm) long and ½ to ¾ inch (1.3 to 1.7 cm) thick

2 ounces (60 g) prosciutto, sliced paper-thin

You can't get more basic than meatloaf. And there's nothing wrong with that. But, as we so often do, we wanted to see how far we could go with this most comforting and common element of our national cuisine. Sure, it's a fun challenge. But our end goal is delicious food. Yeah, it's a little luxe. But you're worth it.

To make the meatloaf: Prepare smoker and bring heat to 325°F, or preheat oven to 325°F (170°C, or gas mark 3).

Place the dried porcini in a bowl of hot water and let rehydrate for 10 minutes. Strain, saving 1 cup (235 ml) liquid for sauce. Refrigerate reconstituted mushrooms for 10 minutes.

Using the grinder attachment on a stand mixer, grind the beef, veal, and porcini. Place in a bowl, cover, and refrigerate immediately.

Heat 2 tablespoons (30 ml) of the oil in a heavy-bottomed sauté pan over medium heat. Stir in the onion, garlic, and rosemary and cook for 8 to 10 minutes, until the onions are translucent. Cool to room temperature.

In a bowl, combine the onion mixture with the tomato paste, panko, eggs, ½ cup (120 ml) of the ketchup, Worcestershire sauce, and milk, and mix well. Using a wooden spoon, stir in the ground meat until fully incorporated. Season with salt and pepper.

At this point, we suggest sautéing a small piece of the ground meat mixture to taste for seasoning. Heat the remaining 1 tablespoon (15 ml) vegetable oil in a small sauté pan over medium-high heat. Break off a 2-tablespoon (30-ml) piece of ground meat and sear 2 minutes per side. Taste, and adjust seasonings if necessary.

FOR SAUCE:

1 cup (235 ml) reserved mushroom liquid

1 tablespoon (15 ml) ketchup

½ cup (120 ml) heavy cream

2 tablespoons (16 g) flour

1 teaspoon (5 ml) Worcestershire sauce

1½ ounces (45 g) black truffles, shaved (canned is fine)

Kosher salt and freshly cracked black pepper, to taste

SPECIAL EQUIPMENT:

Grinder attachment to stand mixer

On a greased baking sheet, shape half of the remaining meat into a 5 × 9-inch (13 × 23-cm) rectangle, about ½ inch (1.3 cm) thick. Place the strip of foie gras (**A**) down the center lengthwise, then mound the rest of the meat around it, forming a loaf. Schmear with remaining ¼ cup (60 ml) ketchup, then lay the prosciutto over the loaf so the slices overlap by about ½ inch (1.3 cm).

Place the loaf into the smoker or oven, and smoke or bake for 45 to 50 minutes, or until the internal temperature of the foie gras registers 140°F (60°C). Remove from smoker or oven and let rest for at least 10 minutes. Using an offset spatula, transfer the loaf to a cutting board, reserving the juices on the baking sheet (**B**).

To make the sauce: In a small bowl, combine the reserved mushroom liquid, ketchup, and heavy cream, and set aside. Place the reserved drippings in a 1-quart (946-ml) saucepan over medium heat and stir with a fork. When they reach a boil, add flour and continue to cook, stirring constantly, for 2 minutes. Slowly stream in the cream mixture, and stir constantly until the flour mixture is fully incorporated. Add the Worcestershire sauce. Simmer gently for 4 minutes, continuing to stir. Add black truffles, then season with salt and pepper.

Slice meatloaf, drizzle sauce over, and serve immediately (**C & D**).

YIELD: 6 to 8 servings

Note: We suggest using a dual-probe remote thermometer, with one end monitoring the temperature in the smoker, and the other in the meatloaf. (See Equipment, page 20.)

A: FOIE GRAS LOBE AND TRUFFLES

B: RESTING LOAF

C: FOIE GRAS INSIDE

D: SHAVED TRUFFLE FOR GARNISH

★ FRIED MAC 'N CHEESE POPS ★

1 pound (455 g) elbow macaroni

½ cup (1 stick, 112 g) butter

4½ cups (562.5 g) flour, divided

1 teaspoon (1.2 g) crushed red pepper flakes

1 teaspoon (6 g) salt

½ teaspoon (1 g) ground black pepper

3½ cups (870 ml) half-and-half

4 cups (460 g) grated Monterey Jack cheese

4½ cups (520 g) bread crumbs, divided

Kosher salt and freshly cracked black pepper, to taste

10 eggs, beaten

6 cups (1.4 L) vegetable oil, for frying

SPECIAL EQUIPMENT:

45 wooden Popsicle sticks, deep fryer or deep saucepan (you will need to hold about 2 inches [5 cm] of oil)

Every year, at Harpoon's Championship of New England Barbecue in Windsor, Vermont, we have the chance to be vendors as well as competitors. This dish is by far one of our most popular. It's a little time-consuming, but it's absolutely worth it. Before you begin, make sure you have space in your freezer, because these have to stay frozen until they are fried. If you don't need the full batch for your gathering (or if you'd like to double the recipe to keep these on hand!), freeze the remaining pops in an airtight container for up to four weeks, and fry them as needed.

In a large pot of boiling, salted water, cook macaroni according to package directions. Drain very well, place in a large mixing bowl, and set aside.

In a large saucepan over medium heat, melt the butter. Whisk in ½ cup (62.5 g) of the flour, red pepper flakes, salt, and pepper, stirring constantly until well blended. Continue to cook, stirring, for 2 minutes.

Add half-and-half gradually, whisking constantly. Bring to a boil, stirring often, and cook for 2 minutes. Reduce heat to low and simmer for 10 minutes, stirring often.

Add cheese, ½ cup (57.5 g) at a time, stirring until cheese is melted before adding more. Remove from heat and let cool for 10 minutes. Pour the cheese sauce over the macaroni, add ½ cup (60 g) of the bread crumbs, and mix well. Season with salt and pepper. Cool to room temperature.

Place a piece of waxed paper on a baking sheet. Make forty-five 2-ounce (60-g) balls (about the size of a golf ball) with the macaroni and cheese, and skewer each one with a Popsicle stick. Place in freezer for 20 minutes.

Set up a breading station, with a bowl of the remaining 4 cups (500 g) flour, a bowl of beaten eggs, and a bowl of the remaining 4 cups (460 g) bread crumbs.

Remove macaroni pops from the freezer and bread each one by coating lightly but completely in flour, then egg, then bread crumbs, tapping off excess after each step. Place back on waxed paper and freeze for 30 minutes more. Remove from the freezer and repeat the breading process; freeze again until serving time.

In a deep fryer or deep saucepan, heat the oil to 325°F (170°C). Working in batches of 4 to 6 mac 'n cheese pops, gently lower them one by one into the hot oil and fry until golden brown and heated through, 5 to 7 minutes per batch. The crumbs will brown very quickly, but don't be fooled—it takes a few minutes for the centers to thaw and heat up. It's a good idea to test at least one pop per batch with an instant-read thermometer. It will read 125 to 135°F (51.6 to 57.2°C) when they're done.

Transfer the finished pops to a paper towel–lined plate to drain. Serve immediately, warning guests that the pops are very hot.

YIELD: 45 pops

★ SURF 'N TURF LOBSTER CHOWDER ★

FOR PORK BELLY:

2 tablespoons (30 ml) vegetable oil

2 carrots, peeled and cut into ½-inch (1.3-cm) dice

2 ribs celery, cut into ½-inch (1.3-cm) dice

2 medium onions, chopped

1 quart (946 ml) clam juice

1 quart (946 ml) water or unsalted pork stock

1½ pounds (680 g) pork belly

1 teaspoon (1.2 g) minced fresh rosemary

Usually bacon plays a small role in chowder—a few bits tossed in for flavor. But we wanted to highlight the full beauty of the pork belly. Using the meat's wonderful braising liquid as our base for the chowder adds a great deal of complex flavor to the finished product. In another departure from tradition, we pour hot water over lobsters in the sink instead of boiling them, because we want to disengage the meat from the shell without overcooking the meat. Reviews on this dish from everyone we've made it for have been unanimous—it's the most delicious lobster chowder they've ever had. We agree. But don't take our word for it. Try it yourself.

To make the pork belly: Prepare smoker and bring temperature to 325°F (170°C).

While smoker is warming, heat the oil in a large sauté pan over medium-high heat. Cook the carrots, celery, and onions until the vegetables start to caramelize, about 10 minutes. Meanwhile, heat clam juice and water in a large saucepan. Bring to a boil, then reduce heat to simmer.

Transfer vegetables to a large Dutch oven with a lid, and place the pork belly in among the vegetables. Pour the hot clam juice mixture over it and add the rosemary.

Cover the Dutch oven and put in smoker for 2½ to 3 hours, or until internal temperature of the pork belly reaches 180°F (82.2°C). Carefully remove pork belly, place on a baking sheet, and refrigerate until needed. Strain the liquid in the Dutch oven, reserving for the chowder.

FOR LOBSTER CHOWDER:

1 to 2 gallons (3.8 to 7.6 L) water, for lobsters

2 lobsters (2 pounds, or 1 kg, each)

1 quart (946 ml) heavy cream

2 sprigs fresh tarragon

3 tablespoons (42 g) butter

1 large onion, chopped

1 rib celery, cut into ¼-inch (6-mm) dice

1 large clove garlic, minced

2 tablespoons (16 g) flour

1 quart (946 ml) reserved pork belly braising liquid

6 new potatoes, cut into ¼-inch (6-mm) dice

Oil, for frying

Kosher salt and freshly cracked black pepper, to taste

To make the lobster chowder: Bring the water to boil in a large pot. Place lobsters on a sheet pan in the sink and pour the boiling water over them, to kill and loosen them from their shells. Let the lobsters cool enough to touch, then separate the tails, knuckles, and claws, and remove the meat from the shells. Cut the tail and claw meat into bite-sized chunks, and set aside. Save the bodies for another use.

Place shells and legs in a heavy-bottomed stockpot with the heavy cream. Bring to a simmer over low heat and maintain a light simmer for 30 minutes. Do not let the cream scorch.

Heat the butter in a large, heavy-bottomed saucepan over medium-low heat. Sweat the onion and celery, stirring frequently, until onion is translucent but not browned, 5 to 10 minutes. Add the garlic and cook for 1 minute. Sprinkle the flour evenly over vegetables and cook for about 3 minutes, stirring constantly.

Strain the cream from the lobster shells. Add about half the cream to the saucepan with the onion and celery, and stir vigorously to incorporate until cream is smooth. Add the rest of the cream and repeat. Add braising liquid and simmer. Increase heat to medium, add the potatoes, and simmer for about 15 minutes, until potatoes are almost tender.

In a deep sauté pan, heat oil to 350°F (180°C). Cut the braised pork belly into 1-inch (2.5-cm) cubes. Deep-fry belly squares for 2 to 4 minutes, until golden brown and the skin is blistering. Remove from pan and place on paper towels to drain.

Add the reserved lobster meat to the chowder, stirring quickly. Season with salt and pepper.

Ladle about ½ inch (1.3 cm) of chowder into 6 flat-bottom bowls, then place the pork belly in the center. Serve immediately.

YIELD: 6 servings

★ HICKORY-SMOKED BEEF ON WECK ★

FOR HICKORY-SMOKED BEEF:

One 9- to 10-pound (4- to 4.5-kg) beef chuck shoulder roast

½ cup (50 g) Dalmatian Rub (page 139)

1 cup (235 ml) Beef BBQ Marinade (page 46)

Whenever we find ourselves in upstate New York for barbecue contests, we don't go looking for the ubiquitous Buffalo wings, like everybody else. If we're not eating our own barbecue, we save our appetites for the local specialty, beef on weck. Said to have originated in Buffalo, this oddly named dish is basically a roast beef sandwich. The fun part of the name comes from the bread it's served on—a kimmelweck roll, which is like a Kaiser roll topped with caraway seeds and pretzel salt. It's usually served with horseradish, pickles on the side, and a tall one. Here is our take, with a barbecue twist. The long cook time (very little of which requires active participation) gives the meat a sweet smoky flavor, crisp bark, and super tenderness that elevate it to a very different level than what you find in a traditional roast beef sandwich.

To make the hickory-smoked beef: Rub meat all over with Dalmatian Rub.

Prepare smoker and bring heat to 250°F (120°C). Use hickory wood for flavor.

Smoke beef until it registers an internal temperature of 165°F (73.8°C), about 6 hours.

Lay two pieces of aluminum foil, long enough to wrap around meat, on top of each other. Transfer meat from the smoker to the foil, pour marinade over it, and wrap tightly in foil. Return to the smoker until meat reaches an internal temperature of 190°F, about 3 hours more. Remove meat from smoker, unwrap foil, and place in a baking dish. Pour the accumulated juices over the meat. We like to cool it to room temperature, then refrigerate, covered, overnight. You can just let it rest for a short time and slice for sandwiches right away, but the meat is so tender that it is much easier to slice after it has been refrigerated.

FOR HORSERADISH CREAM SAUCE:

½ cup (115 g) mayonnaise

½ cup (115 g) sour cream

6 tablespoons (90 g) prepared horseradish

1 tablespoon (15 ml) Dijon mustard

1 tablespoon (3 g) chopped chives

½ teaspoon (0.9 g) cayenne pepper

Juice of ½ lemon

FOR KIMMELWECK ROLLS:

1 cup (235 ml) water

2 tablespoons (16 g) cornstarch

16 Kaiser rolls

½ cup (150 g) sea salt

½ cup (50 g) caraway seeds

To make the horseradish cream sauce: In a medium bowl, whisk mayonnaise, sour cream, horseradish, mustard, chives, cayenne, and lemon juice. Cover and refrigerate until needed.

To make the kimmelweck rolls: In a small saucepan over medium heat, bring water and cornstarch to a boil. Reduce heat to low and stir until the mixture thickens. Remove from heat and let cool. Brush each roll with the cornstarch mixture and sprinkle liberally with sea salt and caraway seeds.

To serve, preheat oven to 300°F (150°C, or gas mark 2). Remove beef chuck roast from the refrigerator and slice thinly. Place pieces back into the baking dish with the reserved juices. Cover and warm in oven for 20 minutes. Stack warm beef on rolls, drizzle with pan juices, spoon on some horseradish sauce, and serve.

YIELD: 16 generous sandwiches

★ BBQ SCOTCH EGGS ★

6 eggs, at room temperature

2 pounds (1 kg) pork sausage, casings removed

½ cup (120 ml) maple syrup

½ cup (50 g) IQUE Dry Rub (page 32)

This is a gastropub standard that we like to serve for breakfast after a long night of tending the fire in our barbecue pit. You can do the prep work for this dish while other things are cooking, so everything is ready to go as soon as your smoker has room. A lot of recipes call for hard-cooked eggs wrapped in sausage meat and then deep-fried. We prefer ours soft cooked. You may need to experiment with the cooking time of the eggs, with the goal being fully cooked whites and yolks that are just slightly runny. We call for 3 minutes, but variables like the size of the eggs may impact your timing. We also skip the deep-frying and use our barbecue pit to smoke the sausage, which gives it a sweet, smoky taste, and ensures that the yolks of the soft-cooked eggs will stay soft. We suggest you do the same.

Place eggs in a saucepan with enough cold water to cover. Bring to a boil over high heat, then lower heat so water simmers very gently for 3 minutes. Remove eggs from the water with a slotted spoon and carefully plunge into an ice-water bath. After 10 minutes, carefully remove the shells. Refrigerate for 2 hours or overnight. Carefully remove the shells under cold running water.

In a bowl, mix the sausage and maple syrup. Divide into 6 even portions and form into balls. Flatten each ball into a roughly 5-inch (13-cm) circle, about ¼ inch (6 mm) thick, on parchment or waxed paper. Place an egg in the center of the circle and mold the sausage around the egg with your hands (A & B). Sprinkle generously with IQUE Dry Rub and refrigerate on a small sheet pan for 1 hour or overnight.

A: PLACE EGG IN CENTER OF SAUSAGE AND MOLD SAUSAGE AROUND IT.

B: PRESS ENDS OF SAUSAGE TO SEAL.

C: SMOKED SCOTCH EGG.

BBQ SCOTCH EGGS (CONTINUED)

Prepare smoker and bring temperature to 250°F (120°C). Place the baking sheet with the scotch eggs on the smoker for 1 hour, or until the internal temperature of sausage meat reaches 165°F (73.8°C) (**c**).

Serve immediately with multigrain toast or, if you're feeling really sinful, Fire-Cooked Cornbread (page 106) and Honey Butter (page 109).

YIELD: 6 servings

★ FIRE-COOKED CORNBREAD ★
WITH BACON JAM AND HONEY BUTTER

1 pound (455 g) sliced bacon

2 cups (275 g) cornmeal

1½ cups (187.5 g) flour

2 tablespoons (27.6 g) baking powder

2 teaspoons (8 g) sugar

1 teaspoon (6 g) salt

2 cups (475 ml) buttermilk

3 eggs

1 tablespoon (14 g) butter, at room temperature

1 teaspoon (3.6 g) sea salt flakes

Bacon Jam (recipe follows)

Honey Butter (recipe follows)

Up north we see a lot of sweet, cakey cornbread, but we definitely prefer the Southern version, which is more dense, savory, and often cooked in a preheated cast-iron skillet to get that nice crispy crust. A bit of bacon fat doesn't hurt, either. We take things a bit further and also introduce bacon to jam, a match made in heaven. Add soft honey butter, and you have a righteous picnic food. For a holy trinity of pig, match this up with pulled pork. After enjoying this combination, you should probably think about booking some time at the gym.

In a well-seasoned 10- to 12-inch (25- to 30-cm) cast-iron pan, fry bacon over medium-high heat until crisp. Drain it well, pouring the fat into a bowl. Chop the bacon and set aside. Reserve pan.

Prepare smoker or grill and bring temperature to 350°F (180°C).

While the grill is heating, in a large bowl, combine the cornmeal, flour, baking powder, sugar, and salt, and whisk to combine. In another bowl, whisk the buttermilk and eggs to blend.

Place the reserved pan on the grill grate, and brush any residual fat left in the pan evenly over the bottom and sides. (If you need any more fat to coat the pan, take it from the bowl.) Discard excess fat or reserve it for future use.

While the pan is heating, pour the buttermilk mixture into the dry ingredients and mix the batter together using as few strokes as possible. Fold in the chopped bacon, and pour the batter into the hot pan, smoothing the surface. Cook for 30 minutes. Brush the top of the cornbread with butter and sprinkle with sea salt. Return to cook until a toothpick inserted into the center comes out clean, 6 to 8 minutes more.

Transfer the cornbread to a wire rack to cool for 10 minutes. Gently tip the cornbread out onto a cutting board, and use a large, sharp knife to cut the bread into wedges. Return the cornbread wedges to the cast-iron pan to keep warm, and serve immediately with Bacon Jam and Honey Butter.

YIELD: One 10- or 12-inch (25- or 30-cm) round, or 8 to 10 servings

BACON JAM

2 pounds (1 kg) sliced bacon

1 large sweet onion, sliced

4 cloves garlic, chopped

3 tablespoons (22.5 g) IQUE Dry Rub (page 32)

½ cup (120 ml) cider vinegar

½ cup (120 ml) whiskey

½ cup (120 ml) maple syrup

5 tablespoons (75 g) light brown sugar

2 tablespoons (30 ml) hot sauce

As delicious as this jam is with our cornbread, it also has the potential to be your "secret spread." Try it with Buttermilk Slider Rolls (page 71), Grandma Wolff's Super Smoked Scrapple (page 186), or simply on toast, with eggs cooked any style.

In a 12-inch (30-cm) sauté pan over medium-high heat, fry bacon until crisp but not too well done. Drain the bacon, reserving 2 tablespoons (30 ml) fat in the pan. Chop and set aside.

Add the onion to the pan with the reserved bacon fat and cook over medium heat, stirring often, until the onion is very soft and deep golden brown, 20 to 30 minutes.

Add the garlic and IQUE Dry Rub to the pan, stirring to coat the onions, and cook 3 minutes more, until fragrant. Add the vinegar, whiskey, syrup, sugar, and hot sauce and bring to a boil, scraping up all the browned bits stuck to the pan. Lower the heat so the mixture simmers gently until it is thick and sticky, about 1 hour. Cool to room temperature.

Using a rubber spatula, transfer to a food processor fitted with the steel blade, and pulse just until the bacon becomes a thick, jammy mass.

Bacon Jam will keep, covered and refrigerated, for up to 2 weeks.

YIELD: 2 cups (470 ml)

HONEY BUTTER

1 cup (2 sticks, 225 g) unsalted butter, cut into chunks

½ cup (120 ml) honey

1 tablespoon (3.6 g) coarse sea salt

In a food processor fitted with a steel blade, blend the butter and honey until smooth. Pulse in the sea salt.

Pile the butter onto a sheet of waxed paper or plastic wrap. Roll it up into a log, twisting ends tightly to seal and shape the log. Refrigerate for up to 2 weeks.

YIELD: 2 cups (450 g)

★ COLOSSAL BBQ SHRIMP ★ WITH CRAB CAKE STUFFING

FOR BRINE:

3 cups (750 ml) water

½ cup (150 g) kosher salt

½ cup (75 g) packed brown sugar

3 bay leaves

2 tablespoons (10 g) white peppercorns

8 giant shrimp, 3 to 4 ounces (85 to 115 g) each (U4)

FOR CRAB CAKE STUFFING:

1½ medium carrots, peeled and cut into ¼-inch (6-mm) dice

1½ ribs celery, cut into ¼-inch (6-mm) dice

1 medium onion, cut into ¼-inch (6-mm) dice

1 tablespoon (10 g) minced garlic

2 tablespoons (28 g) unsalted butter

¼ cup (60 g) mayonnaise

Zest of 4 lemons

1 tablespoon (2.4 g) chopped fresh thyme

¼ cup (15 g) finely chopped fresh parsley

2 teaspoons (5.2 g) Old Bay Seasoning

1 cup (115 g) panko or bread crumbs

2 cups (236 g) lump crabmeat

Kosher salt and freshly cracked black pepper, to taste

IQUE Hollandaise Sauce (recipe follows)

1 tablespoon IQUE Dry Rub (page 32)

We've made this winning recipe for many competitions, and since we know that people—in this case, the judges—eat with their eyes first, we like to use really big shrimp. In industry speak, your standard cocktail-size shrimp is called a 16/20, which means 16 to 20 per pound, with each one weighing 1 ounce (28 g) or less. Here we call for U4, meaning there are under (U) four per pound. They are bigger than jumbo shrimp, our favorite oxymoron. Order shrimp this size from your local fishmonger. This dish comes together relatively quickly, and the results are spectacular. You will probably have extra stuffing, which makes delicious crab cakes, mixes well with scrambled eggs, and is delicious on toast, for a variation on shrimp toasts.

To make the brine: In a large saucepan over high heat, bring the water, salt, sugar, bay leaves, and peppercorns to a rolling boil. Remove from heat and cool until it reaches a temperature lower than 41°F (5°C).

Remove the shells of the shrimp, leaving the tail on, and devein them from the belly side (see sidebar, page 113). Place the shrimp in the brine with 2 cups (475 ml) ice and keep cold. Brine for 25 minutes. Drain and pat dry.

To make the crab cake stuffing: In a sauté pan over medium-low heat, cook carrots, celery, onion, and garlic in the butter until tender, 5 to 10 minutes. Remove from heat and let cool. Transfer to a bowl and stir in mayonnaise, lemon zest, thyme, parsley, Old Bay Seasoning, and panko. Gently fold in the crabmeat, trying to keep the chunks intact (we like to really see the crab). Season with salt and pepper.

Prepare smoker and bring temperature to 300°F (150°C).

A: STARTING FROM THE TAIL, MAKE AN
INCISION THROUGH THE SHRIMP'S BELLY.

B: POSITION STUFFING INSIDE THE SHRIMP,
THEN WRAP TAIL UP AND OVER IT.

C: IF YOU DON'T WANT TO USE A BAKING
DISH OR SHEET PAN, PLACE SHRIMP
DIRECTLY ON THE SMOKER GRATE.

COLOSSAL BBQ SHRIMP WITH CRAB CAKE STUFFING (CONTINUED)

While the smoker is heating, stuff the shrimp. Place about ½ cup (120 ml) of stuffing in your hands and shape into an oval. Position inside a shrimp, wrapping the tail up and over it (B). Repeat with remaining shrimp.

Place the shrimp in a buttered 9 × 12-inch (23 × 30-cm) baking dish or sheet pan, or directly on the smoker grate, and smoke for 8 to 10 minutes, until the shrimp are pink and no longer translucent, or until an instant-read thermometer inserted in the meat of the shrimp registers 145°F (62.7°C). Remove from the smoker (C).

To serve, arrange shrimp on a serving platter, drizzle with IQUE Hollandaise Sauce, and sprinkle with IQUE Dry Rub.

YIELD: 8 servings

IQUE HOLLANDAISE SAUCE

2 cups (475 ml) water

3 egg yolks

1 tablespoon (15 ml) fresh lemon juice

¾ cup (1½ sticks, 167 g) unsalted butter, cut into small cubes

2 teaspoons (10 ml) Tabasco sauce

1 tablespoon (7.5 g) IQUE Dry Rub (page 32)

In a medium saucepan over medium heat, bring the water to a boil. Lower heat and reduce to a simmer. In a metal mixing bowl large enough to sit over the saucepan, whisk yolks and lemon juice until yolks lighten in color, 2 to 3 minutes. Place the bowl over the saucepan, and whisk constantly until mixture thickens, 3 to 5 minutes (it should coat the back of a spoon). Remove from heat and, whisking constantly, add butter, 1 cube at a time, making sure each one is blended in before adding another. When all the butter is incorporated, whisk in Tabasco sauce and IQUE Dry Rub. Reserve until shrimp are ready.

BELLY UP

GENERALLY, SHRIMP ARE DEVEINED FROM THE BACK. FOR PRESENTATION, WE LIKE TO DO IT FROM THE BELLY. IT'S A LITTLE TOUGHER, BUT THE SHRIMP LOOK BETTER. TO DEVEIN THE SHRIMP WHILE KEEPING THE BACK INTACT, USE THIS CHALLENGING TECHNIQUE:

USING A SHARP PARING KNIFE, STARTING FROM THE TAIL, MAKE AN INCISION THROUGH THE SHRIMP'S BELLY, ALMOST BUT NOT COMPLETELY THROUGH TO THE OTHER SIDE, BEING CAREFUL NOT TO PIERCE THE BACK (A). THEN BUTTERFLY THE SHRIMP ALL THE WAY TO THE HEAD. OPEN IT UP AND REMOVE THE VEIN.

★ D.I.Y. CORNDOGS ★

FOR HOT DOGS:

2 pounds (1 kg) pork butt, with fat,
cut into ½-inch (1.3-cm) strips

2 pounds (1 kg) beef chuck, with fat,
cut into ½-inch (1.3-cm) strips

1½ teaspoons (9 g) salt

1 tablespoon (7 g) mild paprika

1 tablespoon (6 g) ground white pepper

1 teaspoon (6 g) Prague Powder #1,* optional
(see Resources, page 218)

1 teaspoon (3 g) mace

1 teaspoon (3 g) garlic powder

¼ cup (60 ml) cold water

When we were kids, corndogs were one of those rare treats we only got once a year or so, when the fair came through town. When we got older, we set out to make the best corndog we could—at home. Everything tastes better when you make it yourself, and often, it's better for you. So now, you can wait for the fair to come to town. Or you can take matters into your own hands.

To make the hot dogs: Season meat with salt, and freeze until stiff but not frozen, about 1 hour. We recommend putting the grinder attachments in the freezer with the meat. This inhibits bacteria growth, keeps the meat and fat emulsified during grinding, and makes it easier to grind the meat.

Remove meat from the freezer and grind it, using the medium grinder plate. Return to freezer for 20 minutes, with the grinder attachments. After 20 minutes, remove from freezer and grind again, this time using the fine grinder plate. Refrigerate.

Prepare smoker and bring heat to 200°F (93°C).

While smoker is heating, place paprika, white pepper, Prague Powder (if using), mace, and garlic powder in a spice grinder and process until finely ground. Transfer to a small bowl, and dissolve spices in the cold water.

In the bowl of a food processor, mix the meat and spices and process until fully combined.

Shape 2-ounce (55-g) portions of the meat mixture into 32 mini hot dogs, about 3 inches (7.5 cm) long.

Insert sticks about three-quarters of the way into each dog. Arrange dogs on a baking sheet lined with parchment paper and smoke for 20 to 30 minutes, or until the internal temperature reaches 140°F (60°C). Remove from smoker and let cool.

FOR BATTER:

4 cups (550 g) cornmeal

2 cups (250 g) flour

2 teaspoons (9.2 g) baking soda

1 teaspoon (6 g) salt

2 teaspoons (5 g) ground cumin

¼ cup (50 g) sugar

2 eggs

2½ cups (570 ml) buttermilk

1½ cups (355 ml) water

1 pound (455 g) Tasso ham or
applewood-smoked bacon, diced very small

Peanut or vegetable oil, for frying

2 cups (250 g) flour

Spicy Mustard (recipe follows)

SPECIAL EQUIPMENT:

Grinder attachment to stand mixer,
32 Popsicle sticks, deep fryer

To make the batter: In a medium bowl, combine cornmeal, flour, baking soda, salt, cumin, and sugar. In a separate bowl, beat the eggs, then stir in buttermilk and water. Using a wooden spoon, stir wet ingredients into dry, being careful not to overwork. Fold in diced ham.

Pour oil into deep fryer and heat to 350°F (180°C). Pour flour on a plate.

One by one, holding the end of the stick, roll the smoked hot dogs in the flour to coat. Working in batches of 4 to 6 at a time, dip the hot dogs in the batter, let some of the excess drip off, then lower them into the hot oil, holding onto the ends of the sticks. Keep them in the oil for 15 seconds, holding them so the corndog does not touch the bottom or sides of frying apparatus.

Release the corndogs into the fryer and fry for 4 to 6 minutes, until golden brown. Cool the corndogs on a plate lined with paper towels for 2 to 4 minutes, then serve with mustard.

YIELD: 32 corndogs

Note: Prague Powder #1, also known as pink or curing salt, is made up of 6.25 percent sodium nitrate and 93.75 percent sodium chloride. It is used to cure meat and can be used as a dry rub cure.

SPICY MUSTARD

2 cups (470 ml) yellow mustard

1 tablespoon (5.3 g) cayenne pepper

1 tablespoon (15 ml) pickle juice

1 tablespoon (15 g) turbinado sugar

Combine all ingredients in a bowl and mix well.

YIELD: 2 cups (470 ml)

★ BBQ GRAVY FRIES ★ WITH STINKY CHEESE SAUCE

FOR FRIES:

6 to 8 large russet potatoes, peeled

Peanut or vegetable oil, for frying

FOR BBQ GRAVY:

2 tablespoons (28 g) unsalted butter

2 tablespoons (16 g) flour

1½ cups (355 ml) Smoked Pork Stock (recipe follows) or low-sodium chicken broth

1½ cups (355 ml) Basic Pulled Pork (recipe follows)

Kosher salt and freshly cracked black pepper, to taste

IQUE Dry Rub, optional (page 32)

¾ cup (175 ml) Stinky Cheese Sauce (recipe follows)

½ cup (60 g) crumbled blue cheese

¼ cup (12 g) minced chives

SPECIAL EQUIPMENT:

Deep fryer

Try putting these in the middle of your poker table at 3 a.m. after an evening of imbibing. It is our take on poutine, the culinary curiosity that made its way south from Montreal and captured our collective imaginations. You can make the BBQ Gravy and Stinky Cheese Sauce in advance so the recipe comes together quickly for late-night snack attacks. In the morning, much may be forgotten about the previous evening's activities, but most certainly not the BBQ Gravy Fry experience.

To make the fries: Cut the potatoes into ¼-inch-thick (6-mm) fries, and soak in a bowl of cold water for 30 minutes to an hour.

Fill the deep fryer with oil and bring oil to 275°F (140°C).

While the oil is heating, make the BBQ Gravy: In a large frying pan over medium heat, combine the butter and flour. Lower heat and continue to cook, stirring often, for 10 minutes. Add the stock, increase heat, and bring to a boil. Reduce heat and simmer for 15 minutes. Stir in pulled pork, and keep warm. Taste and adjust seasoning with salt, pepper, and IQUE Dry Rub, if desired.

Remove potatoes from water and dry on paper towels. Transfer to deep fryer and fry until they just begin to color, about 3 to 5 minutes. Remove and drain in the deep fryer's basket. Transfer to a baking pan until ready to serve.

Increase temperature of the fry oil to 375°F (190°C). Return potatoes to the fryer and fry until browned and crispy, about 3 minutes more. Season with salt, pepper, and IQUE Dry Rub.

Arrange fries on a serving platter and ladle a generous portion of the BBQ Gravy over them. Drizzle with Stinky Cheese Sauce, and sprinkle crumbled blue cheese and chives over the top.

YIELD: 4 to 8 servings

SMOKED PORK STOCK

8 pounds (3.64 kg) fresh pork hocks, pigs' feet, rib trimmings, or a mix

2 large sweet onions, unpeeled, sliced into 1-inch (2.5-cm) rounds

2 carrots, peeled and cut into 1-inch (2.5-cm) chunks

2 ribs celery, chopped

6 to 8 sprigs curly parsley

This is a very versatile ingredient to have in your refrigerator or freezer. Rich and smoky, it can elevate all sorts of dishes, from soups to gravy. If you are not a big fan of barbecue sauces, this is a great way to add moisture and flavor to pulled pork.

Prepare smoker and bring temperature to 225°F (107°C).

Smoke pork pieces for 3 hours, or until the meat registers an internal temperature of 195°F (90°C) and pulls away from the bone easily. At this point you can continue making the stock, or cool pork to room temperature until ready to use.

Place the smoked pork in a 5-quart (4.7-L) pot and cover with the sliced onions, carrots, and celery. Fill pot with enough cold water to cover all the ingredients. Bring to a boil, then reduce heat to a slow simmer. Sprinkle parsley over the stock. Gently simmer for 4 hours, skimming any foam from the top, especially during the first hour. Where the stock reduces, let a raft form below a crust of onion, parsley, and the slightly exposed pork shanks. Do not disturb the raft, as it acts to clarify the stock.

In a very large bowl, prepare an ice bath. Place a 4-quart (3.8-L) bowl in it and place a strainer lined with cheesecloth over the larger bowl. Very slowly, pour the stock through the strainer, leaving a few inches of it in the pot—that remaining stock contains impurities that will make it cloudy.

While the stock is cooling, whisk it periodically to release steam. Cool stock to room temperature, then refrigerate, uncovered, overnight. Stock will keep refrigerated, covered, for up to 5 days, or frozen for up to 2 months.

YIELD: 6 cups (1.4 L)

BASIC PULLED PORK

One 8-pound (3.64-kg) bone-in pork butt

1 cup (100 g) IQUE Dry Rub (page 32)

½ cup (120 ml) Pork Marinade Sauce (page 32)

This recipe makes more pulled pork than you will need for the BBQ Gravy Fries, but consider it a bonus. The pork freezes well, and you can use it for loads of different dishes. We like to stir it into a finished pot of greens or beans, add it to omelets, load it onto baked potatoes, and make pulled pork nachos or enchiladas. You're really limited only by your imagination. You might want to freeze it in a few smallish portions, so you can pull it out and defrost just the amount you will need for whatever you are making.

———————————————————————

Rinse the pork butt, but do not trim any of the fat. Generously apply IQUE Dry Rub all over meat, wrap tightly in plastic wrap, and refrigerate for 4 to 6 hours.

Unwrap the pork butt and let sit at room temperature for up to an hour.

Prepare smoker and heat to 250°F (120°C). Place pork butt on the smoker, fat-side up, close the lid, and crack a beer. Smoke pork for 6 hours, or until the internal temperature reaches 175°F (79°C). Flip the butt fat-side down. Smoke until internal temperature registers 195°F (90°C), about 2 more hours. If the pork is not done after 2 hours, wrap tightly in aluminum foil until it reaches 195°F (90°C). It is helpful at this stage to monitor the internal temperature with a probe thermometer.

Remove pork from smoker and place into a pan fat-side up. Pour the marinade over the pork, tent with foil, and let it rest for 1 hour. Pull pork into large, thumb-sized chunks, mixing the meat with the accumulated juices in the pan. Serve immediately or refrigerate, wrapped, for up to 3 days.

YIELD: About 8 cups (1.9 L), or 10 servings

STINKY CHEESE SAUCE

1 tablespoon (14 g) unsalted butter

1 tablespoon (7 g) flour

1 cup (235 ml) whole milk

¼ pound (115 g) Epoisses, Raclette, or Morbier, rind removed and cut into large pieces

In a medium saucepan over medium heat, melt butter. Add flour and stir for 1 to 2 minutes. Pour in milk, bring to a low simmer, and whisk for 2 minutes. Stir in the cheese. Reduce heat to low and continue to cook, stirring, until sauce thickens. Serve immediately.

YIELD: 1 cup (235 ml)

★ MINTED MOLTEN S'MORES CAKE ★

¾ cup (90 g) graham cracker crumbs, plus more for dusting

4 ounces (115 g) bittersweet chocolate chips

4 ounces (115 g) semisweet chocolate chips

1 cup (2 sticks, 225 g) unsalted butter, cubed

6 eggs

1 teaspoon (5 ml) vanilla extract

¼ teaspoon (1.5 g) kosher salt

½ cup (100 g) sugar

1 tablespoon (8 g) flour

Minty Marshmallows (recipe follows)

Chris's kids, Jaimie and Ethan, toast marshmallows off the back of our smoker all the time. Then they make s'mores. Sometimes the adults try to get in on the action, and things have been known to get, shall we say, less than dignified. So we decided to create our own version of this dessert-for-all-ages. It's a play on the now-classic molten chocolate cake. If you're not a mint fan, you can make the marshmallows without it, but we strongly recommend trying them with.

Preheat oven to 450°F (230°C, or gas mark 8). Spray two 6-cup muffin pans (or twelve 4-ounce [115-g] disposable aluminum cups) with nonstick spray and dust with graham cracker crumbs.

In the top half of a double boiler set over barely simmering water, melt chocolate chips and butter, stirring occasionally, until chocolate is completely smooth, about 10 minutes. Cool briefly.

In the bowl of a stand mixer with the whisk attachment, beat the eggs, vanilla, salt, and sugar on high until light in color and doubled in volume. Remove from mixer and fold in chocolate mixture and flour. Pour batter into prepared muffin pans or aluminum cups. If using cups, place on baking sheet.

MINTED MOLTEN S'MORES CAKE (CONTINUED)

Now for the real fun: With dampened hands (if they are dry, the marshmallow will stick), take a roughly 2-teaspoon (30-g) piece of marshmallow and roll it into a ball. Push marshmallow ball into the center of a muffin cup, allowing cake batter to cover it. Repeat until all muffin cups have marshmallow.

Bake for 10 to 15 minutes, until the batter starts to puff up but is not completely set. Let cool for 2 minutes. To serve, cover each muffin pan with a baking sheet, then flip over. Tap the bottom of the cakes and lift the tins. The cakes should fall out easily.

Gently transfer to individual serving plates, dust each cake with 1 tablespoon (7.5 g) graham cracker crumbs, and serve immediately.

YIELD: 12 cakes

MINTY MARSHMALLOWS

Powdered sugar, for dusting

5 tablespoons (75 ml) water, divided

½ teaspoon (2.5 ml) peppermint extract

¼ ounce (1 packet, 7.5 g) gelatin powder

¾ cup (150 g) sugar

⅓ cup plus 1 teaspoon (85 ml) light corn syrup

1 vanilla bean, seeds only

SPECIAL EQUIPMENT:

Candy thermometer, pastry brush

This makes more than you'll need for the cakes, but we're guessing that won't be a problem. Cut remaining marshmallow into squares and toss with powdered sugar; store in an airtight container.

Spray bottom and sides of one 5 × 9-inch (13 × 23-cm) loaf pan with nonstick spray, then dust liberally with powdered sugar.

In the bowl of stand mixer fitted with the whisk attachment, combine 3 tablespoons (45 ml) of the water, peppermint extract, and gelatin, and whisk for 10 seconds at medium speed. Let stand while you make the syrup.

In a small, heavy-bottomed saucepan over medium heat, bring remaining 2 tablespoons (30 ml) water, sugar, corn syrup, and vanilla bean seeds to a boil, stirring frequently, until the sugar is dissolved. Place a candy thermometer in the liquid and continue to boil until it reaches 240°F (115°C), about 7 to 10 minutes. While this is coming to temperature, brush the sides of the pan with a damp (but not wet) pastry brush to remove any crystals forming on the side of the pan, but do not stir.

With electric mixer set at low speed, slowly pour hot syrup into the gelatin mixture in a thin stream. When half of the liquid has been added, increase the mixer speed to medium and continue pouring. Once all of the liquid has been added, increase speed to high and whisk until it is light, fluffy, and tripled in volume, about 10 minutes. (It should look like meringue meets marshmallow fluff.)

With a rubber spatula, spread marshmallow into prepared loaf pan. Smooth the top and dust with powdered sugar. Loosely cover with plastic wrap and let set for at least 10 hours at room temperature. Cut into squares.

YIELD: About 18 1½-inch (3.8-cm) square marshmallows

★ PECAN PIE–STUFFED CHEESECAKE ★

Remember that old commercial where two people accidentally run into each other—one is holding a chocolate bar and one has some peanut butter—and behold(!), the world has peanut butter cups? Well, this dessert is kind of like that. Except it was no accident. For years, our IQUE teammate Ed Doyle had urged us to come up with the perfect pecan pie–stuffed cheesecake. We've had many discussions about how to make it and many attempts at getting it just right. This one, in which the cheesecake is refrigerated, rather than baked, is the hands-down winner. People have been known to moan in ecstasy after eating this dessert. Seriously.

PECAN PIE

FOR CRUST:

1½ cups (187.5 g) flour, plus extra for rolling

1 teaspoon (4 g) sugar

½ teaspoon (3 g) salt

½ cup (1 stick, 112 g) very cold unsalted butter, cut into ¼-inch (6-mm) cubes

¼ cup (60 ml) ice water

To make the crust: In a food processor, combine flour, sugar, and salt, and pulse to mix. Add butter and pulse until mixture resembles coarse crumbs. Add ice water, 1 tablespoon (15 ml) at a time, pulsing, until a pinch of crumbly dough sticks to itself. You may not need all of the water.

Remove dough from the food processor onto a clean surface. Knead a few times until dough comes together and can be rolled. Do not over-knead.

Roll dough into a disk about 10 inches (25 cm) in diameter and no more than ⅛ inch (3 mm) thick. Use a little flour if dough is sticking. Carefully drape crust over rolling pin to move to an 8-inch (20-cm) round cake pan. Press gently into the cake pan, and trim crust so that there is no more than ½ inch (1.3 cm) extra around the rim. Chill until firm, about 45 minutes.

Preheat oven to 375°F (190°C, or gas mark 5).

FOR FILLING:

1 cup (110 g) coarsely chopped pecans

½ cup (55 g) pecan halves

½ cup (87.5 g) mini chocolate chips

½ cup (87.5 g) butterscotch or white chocolate chips

1 cup (235 ml) dark corn syrup

2 eggs, lightly beaten

¼ cup (60 g) packed dark brown sugar

¼ cup (60 ml) molasses

2 tablespoons (28 g) unsalted butter, melted

2 tablespoons (16 g) flour

1 teaspoon (5 ml) vanilla extract

½ teaspoon (3 g) salt

SPECIAL EQUIPMENT:

8-inch (20-cm) round cake pan with 1½-inch (3.75-cm) sides (or 2 disposable foil cake pans, doubled up for strength), 3 to 4 cups (555 to 740 g) pie weights (or dried beans, rice, pennies, or salt)

When crust is chilled, line with parchment paper or aluminum foil and fill with weights. Bake for 20 minutes with the weights. Remove from oven, remove weights and parchment or foil, and prick the bottom of the crust several times with a cake tester or fork (but not too many; you don't want any filling to leak through). Return to oven without weights and bake for an additional 8 to 10 minutes, or until crust is light golden. Transfer to a rack and let cool to room temperature.

To make the filling: Place the cooled pie crust on a baking sheet, and put all the pecans and chips in the crust, stirring to distribute evenly. In a bowl, combine the corn syrup, eggs, brown sugar, molasses, butter, flour, vanilla, and salt and whisk to blend. Pour over the pecans and bake until the pie is firm and starting to puff up, about 1 hour. Remove from oven and let cool to room temperature on a wire rack, then refrigerate to cool completely while you make the cheesecake.

YIELD: One 8-inch (20-cm) pie

REFRIGERATOR CHEESECAKE

FOR CRUST:

1 cup (115 g) graham crackers crumbs (from about 6 whole crackers)

½ cup (57.5 g) crispy rice cereal, such as Rice Krispies, lightly crushed

2 tablespoons (30 g) packed light brown sugar

2 tablespoons (26 g) granulated sugar

4 tablespoons (½ stick, 55 g) unsalted butter, melted

1 teaspoon (5 ml) vanilla extract

FOR FILLING:

1 cup (235 ml) heavy cream

16 ounces (455 g) cream cheese, softened

1 cup (235 ml) sweetened condensed milk

¼ cup (60 g) sour cream

¼ cup (60 ml) fresh lemon juice (from 1 large lemon)

2 tablespoons (30 g) finely minced fresh lemon zest (from 1 large lemon)

1 tablespoon (15 ml) vanilla extract

1 teaspoon (4 g) sugar

SPECIAL EQUIPMENT:

9½-inch (23.75-cm) springform pan

To make the crust: Spray a 9½-inch (23.75-cm) springform pan with nonstick spray.

In a bowl, combine the cracker crumbs, cereal, and sugars, mixing well to break up and distribute the brown sugar. Add the butter and vanilla and mix until evenly distributed. Press evenly into the bottom of the prepared pan and set aside.

To make the filling: In the bowl of a stand mixer fitted with the whisk attachment, whip the heavy cream to stiff peaks. Transfer to a small bowl and set aside.

In the same mixer bowl, using the paddle attachment, beat the cream cheese until smooth and creamy. Add the condensed milk, sour cream, lemon juice, zest, vanilla, and sugar and beat on medium speed until evenly blended, scraping sides of bowl as needed. With a large rubber spatula, gently fold in the whipped cream until no white streaks remain.

Spread about 2 cups (475 ml) filling over the graham cracker crust and refrigerate until set, about 1 hour.

Remove the pecan pie from the refrigerator. With a sharp paring knife, cut the pastry along the rim of the pan, so that you can slide the knife between the sides of the pan and the crust all the way around, to loosen it.

Place a baking sheet over the top of the pie, and holding it with one hand on the bottom of the cake pan and one hand on the exact other side on the baking sheet, turn the pie out onto the baking sheet. Place another baking sheet on the bottom of the pie and flip it back over so it is right-side up.

Center the unmolded pecan pie inside the springform pan, pressing lightly to push some of the cheesecake filling toward the sides of the pan. (Make sure the top of the pie sits below the rim of the springform pan.) Spoon more cheesecake filling around the perimeter of the pie, filling the space between the pie and the sides of the pan. Tap the pan gently on the counter to settle the filling and fill any gaps. Spread the remaining filling over the pie to completely enclose it. Refrigerate until completely set and firm, at least 4 hours, preferably overnight.

To serve, run a small, wet knife around the perimeter of the cake, and release the springform ring. Slice with a sharp knife that has been run under hot water and dried. We recommend fresh raspberries and shaved white and dark chocolate to garnish, or a drizzle of Whiskey Caramel Sauce (page 191), but you may have your own, equally fabulous ideas.

YIELD: 10 to 14 servings

★ BACON ALMOND BARK ★ AND BANANA RUM MOUSSE

6 tablespoons (¾ stick, 85 g) unsalted butter

1 cup (200 g) sugar

1 teaspoon (6 g) salt

1½ tablespoons (25 ml) corn syrup

2 tablespoons (30 ml) water

2 cups (350 g) bittersweet chocolate chips

1 cup (175 g) milk chocolate chips

1 cup (145 g) salted almonds, roughly chopped

2 cups (160 g) slab bacon, diced and cooked until golden brown

Banana Rum Mousse (recipe follows)

SPECIAL EQUIPMENT:

Silicone sheet pan liner, candy thermometer

One of our favorite pastry chefs in the United States is Mindy Segal of Mindy's Hotchocolate Restaurant and Dessert Bar in Chicago. We love her cutting-edge creativity, and she generously shared this recipe with us. The bark doesn't have to be served with the mousse (though they are dynamite together). If you have a silicone candy bar mold, you can make candy bars with it, or just enjoy it free-form.

Prepare a baking sheet or jelly-roll pan with a silicone liner.

In a medium, heavy-bottomed saucepan over medium heat, melt the butter. Stir in sugar, salt, corn syrup, and water. Place a candy thermometer in the pan, increase heat to medium-high, and cook, stirring frequently, until temperature reaches 295°F (146°C). Carefully pour onto prepared baking sheet or pan and let cool to room temperature.

In the top half of a double boiler set over barely simmering water, melt chocolate chips, stirring occasionally, until chocolate is completely smooth, about 10 minutes. Remove from heat.

Transfer cooled brittle to a cutting board and chop into roughly dime-sized pieces. They will be all different sizes.

A: MIX ALMONDS AND BACON INTO BRITTLE WITH YOUR HANDS.

B: MELT CHOCOLATE CHIPS IN THE TOP OF A DOUBLE BOILER.

C: POUR HOT, MELTED CHOCOLATE OVER BRITTLE MIXTURE.

Move brittle back to silicone-lined baking sheet, mix in almonds and bacon, and spread everything out over the pan with the palms of your hands (A). Pour the hot, melted chocolate over the mixture, distributing it evenly (B & C). Let cool to room temperature. If it's warm outside, you may want to refrigerate it. When cool and hard, break into big shards.

Mound Banana Rum Mousse in a decorative bowl and place on a platter with "bark" shards scattered around it for dipping.

YIELD: About 7 cups (1.7 L)

BANANA RUM MOUSSE

3 ripe bananas

¼ cup (30 g) powdered sugar

2 tablespoons (30 ml) spiced rum

¼ teaspoon (0.6 g) ground nutmeg

¼ teaspoon (0.6 g) cinnamon

1 cup (115 g) crispy rice cereal, such as Rice Krispies

2 cups (475 ml) heavy cream, whipped to stiff peaks

In a food processor fitted with the steel blade, combine the bananas, powdered sugar, rum, nutmeg, and cinnamon, and process until smooth. Transfer purée to a bowl. Using a rubber spatula, fold in cereal and whipped cream.

Spoon into a serving bowl, cover with plastic wrap, and refrigerate for 1 hour.

YIELD: 8 servings

★ KENNY'S SMOKIN' BUTTER CAKE ★

½ cup (1 stick, 112 g) unsalted butter, at room temperature

4 eggs

1 box (16 ounces, 455 g) pound cake mix

1 pound (455 g) powdered sugar

8 ounces (225 g) cream cheese, at room temperature

Ken Goodman is a man of many talents. One of our IQUE teammates, he shot the photos in this book. AND he developed this cake recipe, which has won us more than a few ribbons in barbecue competitions' desserts category. When perfectly cooked, this cake is crispy and caramelized on the outside, and super moist—almost underdone—inside. You *could* bake it in the oven, but then you'd miss out on all the extra flavor that comes from cooking it in the smoker, over coals. It's your call.

Prepare your smoker and bring temperature to 350°F (180°C). Grease a 9 × 13-inch (23 × 33-cm) baking pan and set aside.

In the bowl of a stand mixer, beat butter, 2 of the eggs, and cake mix until combined. (You can also do this with a spoon.) Using a spatula, spread the batter into the prepared pan and smooth evenly.

In another bowl attached to the stand mixer, beat the powdered sugar, cream cheese, and remaining 2 eggs until smooth. Spread over cake batter.

Place the pan in the smoker and bake, with smoker lid on, for 30 minutes, or until the top is golden and pillowy, and a tester inserted into the cake comes out almost clean. If the temperature in your smoker has dropped too far below 350°F (180°C) during cooking, it may take longer for the cake to finish.

Transfer to a rack to cool. Cut into generous pieces and serve with berries, sliced fruit, or all by its lonesome.

YIELD: 10 to 12 servings

BAKING IN A SMOKER

IF YOU ARE ONE OF THOSE PEOPLE USED TO BAKING IN AN OVEN AND DECIDE TO GO THE SMOKER ROUTE, YOU MAY BE IN FOR A BIT OF A SURPRISE. WHEREAS BAKING IS GENERALLY A VERY PRECISE ACTIVITY, BAKING IN A SMOKER CAN BE LESS SO. DEPENDING ON YOUR LEVEL OF EXPERTISE, YOU MAY HAVE TROUBLE KEEPING YOUR SMOKING TEMPERATURE EXACTLY AT 350°F (180°C). DON'T SWEAT IT. YOUR CAKE JUST MAY TAKE A LITTLE LONGER TO BAKE (MAYBE UP TO 30 MINUTES LONGER). AND IF YOU END UP FINISHING IT IN THE OVEN (AFTER 30 MINUTES ON THE SMOKER, 5 TO 10 MINUTES IN THE OVEN SHOULD DO IT), THERE'S NO SHAME IN THAT. THEN YOU'LL HAVE THE BENEFIT OF THE SMOKY TASTE AND A SHORTER WAIT TIME.

IF YOU BAKE THE CAKE ENTIRELY IN YOUR OVEN, THE SAME TEMPERATURE AND TIMING APPLY, BUT BOTH SHOULD BE EASIER TO CONTROL, PARTICULARLY FOR LESS EXPERIENCED SMOKERS.

★ CHAPTER 5 ★

D.I.Y. BBQ

(FRANKENCUE)

AFTER MANY YEARS OF WORKING in professional kitchens, developing recipes at home, and competing on the barbecue trail, we have a lot of food preparation equipment. But often, everything we have isn't enough. Or everything we have in our home or restaurant kitchen can't be transported outdoors. And we can't buy an outdoor version of our indoor tool. That's cool. We just figure out a way to make what we need. We actually enjoy doing that— we're like mad scientists who figure out how to do what we want by fitting together two disparate pieces of equipment. And, to paraphrase an old saying, our creations are better than the sum of their parts.

For example, when we were competing in the Harpoon Championship of New England BBQ in Windsor, Vermont, in 2003, we had never won the Chef's Choice category. Chef's Choice is an open category in which cooks can generally do whatever they want. Not every competition has that category, but we love it when they do, because it's a chance to be really innovative and show off our talents beyond the Four Mains, which have pretty rigid requirements. When we combine our broad-based culinary expertise with our extensive barbecue skills—two areas you might not think of as complementary—watch out . . .

The first recipe that won this category for us was BBQ Clams Casino. Our primary challenge was figuring out how to recreate a broiler, where the food is heated from above, on our smoker, where the heat source is below the food. Our solution is on page 149, along with our recipe for Make-Your-Own Chorizo and BBQ Clams Casino.

This chapter is all about innovations like our outdoor broiler. It is also about combining classic cooking methods that aren't traditionally used together—like barbecue and sous vide, or smoking and braising—which is another theme common to our Chef's Choice entries. We carry this concept beyond our competitive cooking, to dishes like "Smoke-Vide" Beef Ribs with Blues Hog Foam, which combines smoking and sous vide (cooking vacuum-sealed food in a water bath at a lower temperature for a longer time than in a conventional oven) in a dish that is both high-end and down-home—and, of course, delicious. We've also included what we like to call our Flowerpot Series: food cooked in clay flowerpots, which are simple grilled dishes that take on characteristics of tandoori cooking.

These are all examples of terrific things you can do yourself, building on the basics of barbecue.

★ "SMOKE-VIDE" BEEF RIBS ★ WITH BLUES HOG FOAM

2 "dino-sized" beef short ribs, 2½ pounds (1.14 kg) each, roughly 10 inches (25 cm) long and very meaty (see Note)

2 tablespoons (30 ml) extra-virgin olive oil

½ cup (50 g) Dalmatian Rub (recipe follows)

Blues Hog Foam (recipe follows)

SPECIAL EQUIPMENT:

Vacuum sealer; large (6- to 6½-quart [5.7- to 6.1-L]) slow cooker, preferably one with a temperature probe

In this dish, we marry the down-home American barbecue and high-end sous-vide methods, starting with smoke for flavor and moving on to the vacuum-sealed water bath for 12 to 24 hours. The beauty of sous vide is that after the slow cook is completed, the meat can be held in the bath almost indefinitely. When you are ready to eat, simply pull your dinner out of the water and serve it. Because we are using a fancy method beloved by many high-end chefs, we add a whimsical note with a BBQ sauce foam. It's not something you see every day, but we love mixing the unexpected with classic barbecue dishes.

Prepare your smoker. Bring temperature to 250°F (120°C) and add an assertive smoke wood, such as hickory or pecan.

Brush the ribs with the extra-virgin olive oil and sprinkle liberally with the rub. Smoke for 2 to 3 hours, until internal temperature reaches 155 to 165°F (68 to 74°C).

While the ribs are smoking, prepare the slow cooker. On your stove, heat 5 quarts (4.7 L) water to 170°F (77°C). Transfer the water to the slow cooker and set the temperature to maintain a constant 160°F (71°C). A slow cooker outfitted with a probe works well, but you can experiment with the various settings on your slow cooker in order to maintain the right water temperature. By all means, if you have a professional sous-vide rig with an immersion circulator, use it. But we have found an inexpensive slow cooker does a great job.

Note: Many markets cut beef ribs in half. These may be substituted, but we prefer the whole ribs.

"SMOKE-VIDE" BEEF RIBS WITH BLUES HOG FOAM (CONTINUED)

Remove the ribs from the smoker and vacuum seal them according to manufacturer's instructions. Be sure to get a tight seal. If there are any air pockets, it's time for a do-over. Submerge the vacuum-sealed ribs in the slow cooker and cover. Let the ribs cook for at least 12 and as long as 24 hours.

To serve, remove the ribs from vacuum-sealed pack. Slice the entire piece of beef off of each bone. Carefully slice the beef into ½-inch (1.3-cm) pieces. Fan 4 slices on each plate, then spoon some Blues Hog Foam over the beef. Serve with Collard Chips (page 146), if desired.

YIELD: 4 servings

DALMATIAN RUB

1 cup (300 g) kosher salt

1 cup (300 g) coarsely ground black pepper

3 tablespoons (27 g) garlic granules or garlic powder

1 tablespoon (5.3 g) chipotle powder or cayenne pepper

This is our take on a classic Texas rub. It really lets the beef and smoke flavors shine.

Mix all ingredients in a bowl and store in an airtight container for up to 2 months.

YIELD: 2¼ cups (450 g)

BLUES HOG FOAM

2 cups (475 ml) water

½ cup (125 g) Blues Hog Barbecue Sauce (see Resources, page 218)

1 teaspoon (5 ml) soy lecithin (see Resources, page 218)

2 teaspoons (5.2 g) Blues Hog Dry Rub (see Resources, page 218)

SPECIAL EQUIPMENT:

Immersion hand blender

A good friend of ours, Bill Arnold, invented a fantastic barbecue sauce called Blues Hog. It's very popular on the competition circuit because it has a unique, well-balanced flavor profile. The sauce gets your attention without masking the flavors of the meat. Here we use it as a jumping-off point to elevate the typical barbecue sauce experience. We guarantee this will impress your guests.

Place all ingredients in a shallow mixing bowl. Pulse briefly with an immersion blender just to mix, then pulse for about 1 minute all around the top of the mixture, to create a foam. Spoon the foam into a separate container and discard the remaining liquid.

Spoon the foam over your favorite barbecued meat and sprinkle with additional Blues Hog Dry Rub.

YIELD: 1 cup (235 ml)

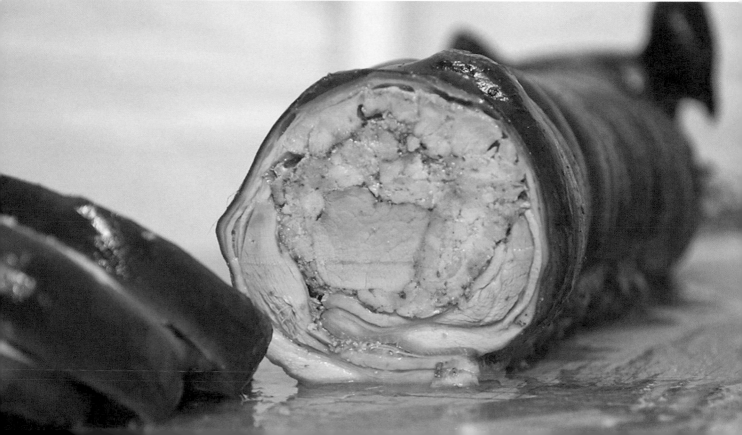

★ WHOLE HOG, PORCHETTA STYLE ★

FOR BRINE:

2 pounds (1 kg) sugar

2 pounds (1 kg) kosher salt,
plus more for seasoning

FOR PORCHETTA:

1 dressed suckling pig, 25 to 30 pounds
(11.4 to 13.7 kg)

Kosher salt and freshly cracked
black pepper, to taste

2 pork tenderloins, about 2 pounds (1 kg) each

1 quart (946 ml) chicken stock

Herb Marinade (recipe follows)

7 pounds (3.2 kg) ground sweet Italian sausage

½ cup (120 ml) vegetable oil

Pork Jus (recipe follows)

Sage leaves for garnish

SPECIAL EQUIPMENT:

5-gallon (18.9-L) food-safe bucket, heavy-duty
aluminum foil, boning knife, butcher's twine

Our good friend and IQUE teammate John Delpha, who owns and operates a great restaurant in Essex, Vermont, called the Belted Cow Bistro, is our Chefs' Choice ringer. John is a two-time winner of the Chefs' Choice category at the Jack Daniel's World Championship Invitational Barbecue competition. His signature dish is a Whole Hog Porchetta. He bones Vermont-raised suckling pigs, stuffs them with wet rub and ground pork, trusses them, and finally smokes them. A whole hog adds festivity to any party. It's not something you'll do every day, but for a special occasion, this dish knocks it out of the park.

To make the brine: In a 5-gallon (18.9-L) food-safe bucket, combine sugar and salt. Add 1 gallon (3.8 L) of very hot water, and stir to dissolve. Add 3 gallons (11.4 L) cold water and stir. Reserve.

To make the porchetta: Cover a 4- to 6-foot (120- to 180-cm) table with heavy-duty aluminum foil. Lay the pig (A) on its back. Holding the head in place, split the pig open, starting at the first rib (B). Using a very sharp, firm-tipped boning knife, separate the ribs from the spine, being careful not to puncture the skin. Follow along the taper of the ribs to cut the bones away from the flesh (C). You want to keep as much meat as possible with the carcass, because this is the part you will be eating. Reserve the bones.

Next, remove the spine, beginning at the neck and working the knife along the vertebrae (D).

A: SUCKLING PIG.

B: SPLIT THE PIG OPEN, STARTING AT THE FIRST RIB.

C: CUT THE BONES AWAY FROM THE FLESH.

WHOLE HOG, PORCHETTA STYLE (CONTINUED)

Once the spine has been removed, carefully remove the hip bones by following the knife around the seams of the surrounding muscles.

Butterfly the legs open (E).

Remove the feet and legs by cutting them off at the first joint (F & G). Season these with salt and pepper and reserve.

Holding the boneless carcass by the head, transfer it, with the pork tenderloins, to the brine and refrigerate for 24 hours.

Prepare smoker and bring heat to 235°F (113°C), using maple and cherry as smoke wood. Place bones and feet on a large sheet pan or in a disposable aluminum roasting pan. Smoke for 1 hour. Remove from smoker, transfer to a large pot, cover halfway with chicken stock, and add enough water to cover pig parts. Simmer over low heat for about 4 hours. Strain, then return to stove and reduce liquid by half. Refrigerate the stock.

Prepare smoker and bring temperature to 250°F (120°C).

Remove the pig and tenderloins from the brine and pat the skin dry. Lay the pig skin-side down on a flat work surface. Rub the inside flesh liberally with the Herb Marinade and season with salt and pepper (H). Rub the tenderloins with the Herb Marinade and toss the ground sausage with some of the Herb Marinade.

Line up the sausage along the cavity of the pig, starting at the neck and working down to the hind legs. Place the tenderloins on top of the sausage, overlapping the thin, pointed ends in the middle.

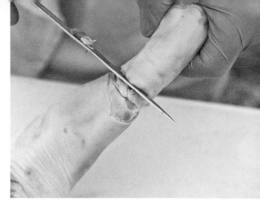

D: REMOVE THE SPINE, BEGINNING AT THE NECK.

E: BUTTERFLY THE LEGS OPEN.

F: CUT LEGS OFF AT FIRST JOINT.

G: CONTINUED.

H: RUB INSIDE OF FLESH WITH HERB MARINADE.

I: TIE EACH OF THE HIND LEGS WITH TWINE.

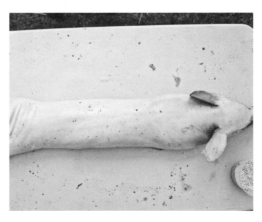

J: ROLL THE PIG LENGTHWISE, OVERLAPPING SKIN TO ENCLOSE THE FILLING.

K: (CONTINUED.)

L: TIE PIECES OF TWINE AROUND THE PIG IN 1-INCH (2.5-CM) INTERVALS.

M: SMOKE FOR 4 TO 4½ HOURS.

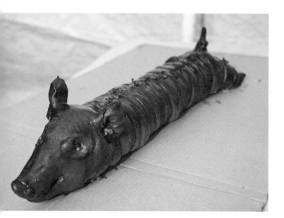

N: SMOKED WHOLE HOG.

O: SLICE 1-INCH (2.5 CM) CROSS SECTIONS OF TORSO.

WHOLE HOG, PORCHETTA STYLE (CONTINUED)

Tie each of the hind legs with three pieces of twine (I). Roll the pig lengthwise, overlapping the skin to completely enclose the filling (J & K). Starting next to the head, tie pieces of twine around the pig in 1-inch (2.5 cm) intervals all the way to the hind legs (L). Tie the hind legs together loosely. Rub the skin, head, and tail with the oil. Season with salt and pepper. Cover the ears and tail with foil.

Smoke pig for 4 to 4½ hours (M), or until the center where the tenderloins are registers approximately 155°F (68°C) (this should mean that the ground pork is about 165°F, or 74°C). Remove from smoker and keep covered in a warm area (N).

To serve: Slice 1-inch (2.5-cm) cross-sections of the torso and thin slices of leg meat on a plate and top with Pork Jus and 1 sage leaf (O).

YIELD: 18 to 22 1-inch (2.5-cm) slices

HERB MARINADE

Leaves from 2 sprigs fresh rosemary, chopped

12 fresh sage leaves

1 bunch curly parsley

5 cloves garlic, crushed

Zest of 1 lemon

1 tablespoon (15 ml) Dijon mustard

5 tablespoons (29 g) freshly ground fennel seed

1½ cups (355 ml) vegetable oil

Combine rosemary, sage, parsley, garlic, lemon zest, mustard, and fennel seed in the bowl of a food processor and pulse until mixture forms a purée. With the machine running, slowly add just enough vegetable oil to form a smooth paste. Transfer marinade to a bowl and add the rest of the oil. Stir to combine; cover. Marinade can be made a day or two in advance and refrigerated.

YIELD: 2 cups (470 ml)

PORK JUS

½ cup (1 stick, 112 g) unsalted butter

12 sage leaves

1 quart (946 ml) Smoked Pork Stock (page 117)

Salt and pepper, to taste

In a medium saucepan over medium heat, stir butter, sage leaves, and Smoked Pork Stock until the butter melts and everything is heated through. Season with salt and pepper, and remove from heat.

YIELD: 1 quart (946 ml)

★ COLLARD CHIPS ★

1½ cups (355 ml) Andy's Famous Collards (page 147), drained well

½ cup (120 ml) water

1 cup (130 g) instant or minute tapioca, finely ground in spice grinder

6 cups (1.4 L) vegetable oil, for frying

Kosher salt or your favorite spice rub (such as IQUE Dry Rub, page 31)

SPECIAL EQUIPMENT:

Deep fryer or deep saucepan (you will need to hold about 2 inches [5 cm] of oil), candy or deep-fry thermometer, food dehydrator (optional)

These chips were developed by our friend Jason Santos, aka "Chef Blue," an amazing chef and runner-up in Season 7 of *Hell's Kitchen*. In the vein of molecular gastronomy, Jason was thinking about how to change collards into something completely different. The chips are puffy, crunchy, and addictive, nothing like roasted collard greens that are sometimes referred to as "chips." To make these, you need to run your oven on just its pilot light or, if that's not possible, use a food dehydrator.

In a food processor, purée collards with water until smooth. Transfer to a bowl and stir in the tapioca to form a stiff, crumbly dough. Divide the dough in half and roll out each piece between two sheets of plastic wrap until it is very thin but not so thin that you can see through it.

Working with one piece at a time, place the rolled-out collards, still covered in plastic wrap, in a flat steamer basket or perforated pan and steam, covered, for 10 minutes. (You can cut the rolled-out pieces to fit into your steamer.) Let cool to room temperature; the collards will have the texture of fruit leather at this point. You can refrigerate the "collard leather" for up to 2 days before proceeding.

When cool, place collard leather, still covered with plastic wrap, on a baking sheet and put in an oven with just the pilot light on for 48 hours, to harden. Alternatively, you can use a food dehydrator for this step: Cut the collard leather into pieces that will fit on the dehydrator trays, and arrange the pieces on the trays without touching. Peel off the top piece of plastic from each piece, and follow the manufacturer's directions to dry.

When the pieces are completely dry, heat the frying oil to 325°F (170°C).

Break the dried collard pieces into 2-inch (5-cm) chips and drop them, a few at a time, into the hot oil. The chips will rise to the surface, looking puffy and light-colored, almost immediately. Turn them over and cook for about 30 seconds total, just until the sizzling starts to subside. Immediately transfer the chips to a paper towel–lined plate, and dust liberally with salt or spice rub. Or dip the chips right into the rub to coat, shaking off excess, as soon as they are cool enough to handle.

Pile the chips in a bowl and enjoy with your favorite beer.

YIELD: About 4 dozen chips

Note: If the chips don't puff up when they hit the fryer, the oil is too cool. Try raising the temperature by 25°F (14°C). If they are not a very bright green, or start to brown, the oil is too hot; lower the temperature by 25°F (14°C).

★ ANDY'S FAMOUS COLLARDS ★

2 medium yellow onions, cut into ½-inch (1.3-cm) dice

6 cloves garlic, minced

¼ pound (115 g) applewood-smoked bacon, cut into ½-inch (1.3-cm) dice

1 cup (235 ml) cider vinegar

¼ cup (60 g) packed brown sugar

¼ cup (60 ml) molasses

1 teaspoon (1.2 g) crushed red pepper flakes

2 bunches collard greens, washed and cut into 1- to 1½-inch (2.5- to 3.75-cm) strips

2 quarts (1.9 L) cold water

Kosher salt and freshly cracked black pepper, to taste

These are always on the menu of Tremont 647, reflecting Andy's long-term love affair with Southern food. They're sweet, spicy, and tart. They only cook for an hour, so the collards retain some texture.

In a large, heavy-bottomed saucepan over medium-high heat, combine all of the ingredients. Bring to a boil, then lower heat to medium. Simmer, stirring occasionally, until the collards are tender, about 45 minutes.

Remove pan from heat. Strain and serve immediately. Or, if you're making Pot Likker and Cornmeal Dumplings (page 151), strain the "pot likker" into a clean saucepan. Be sure to save the collards for Collard Chips (page 146).

YIELD: Serves 6 to 8 as a side dish

★ MAKE-YOUR-OWN CHORIZO ★ AND BBQ CLAMS CASINO

FOR CHORIZO:

¼ pound (115 g) ½-inch (1.3 cm) strips pork shoulder (or ¼ pound [115 g] ground pork)

2 teaspoons (5 g) paprika

2 teaspoons (5.2 g) chili powder

½ teaspoon (0.7 g) dried oregano

1 tablespoon (15 ml) white vinegar

½ jalapeño pepper, stem removed, seeded, and minced (wear gloves)

1 clove garlic, chopped

1 tablespoon (15 ml) canola oil

Kosher salt and freshly cracked black pepper, to taste

FOR CLAMS CASINO:

4 strips smoked bacon, minced

2 teaspoons (10 ml) olive oil

2 slices white bread, toasted to dark brown, then crumbled

2 tablespoons (28 g) butter, room temperature

2 tablespoons (8 g) minced Italian parsley

Zest of 1 lemon, minced

Sea salt, to taste

16 littleneck clams, shucked on the half shell, disconnected but in shell

Lemon wedges and Tabasco sauce, for serving

SPECIAL EQUIPMENT:

Food grinder attachment to stand mixer

In competitions, wood and charcoal are the only heat sources allowed. Once, when the category was shellfish, we decided to make clams casino. We spent a lot of time trying to figure out how to make the necessary wood-fired broiler. We came up with the method below for broiling the clams. Not only did we win the first time we did it, but we've also developed quite a reputation for our ingenuity and our outdoor broiled seafood dishes. Our homemade chorizo may have helped sway the judges in our favor. Like our Sausage Fatties (page 185) and D.I.Y. Corndogs (page 114), we feel the freshness and vibrant flavor that you just can't get in commercial products justify the time it takes to make these Portuguese-inspired sausages. You probably won't want to do it every day, but it's great for impressing guests or slamming the competition.

To make the chorizo: In a bowl, stir together the meat, paprika, chili powder, oregano, vinegar, jalapeño, and garlic. Cover and freeze for about 20 minutes, until meat start to firm. We recommend putting the grinder attachment in the freezer with the meat. This inhibits bacteria growth, keeps the meat and fat emulsified, and makes it easier to grind the meat.

Remove the meat from the freezer. Grind, using the fine plate of the grinder attachment.

Test the flavor of the chorizo: Shape a tablespoon of the ground meat into a flat disk. In a small sauté pan over medium-high heat, cook the patty in the canola oil until golden brown, 1 to 2 minutes per side. Remove from pan, let cool, taste, and season meat mixture with salt and pepper as desired. Refrigerate until needed.

A: HOT COALS ON AN ALUMINUM-LINED RACK ACT AS A "BROILER."

B: CAREFULLY REMOVE CLAMS FROM GRILL.

MAKE-YOUR-OWN CHORIZO AND BBQ CLAMS CASINO (CONTINUED)

To make the clams casino: In a heavy-bottomed sauté pan over medium heat, cook the bacon in the oil, stirring frequently, until crisp, 6 to 8 minutes. Drain on paper towels.

When the bacon is cool, transfer to a bowl. Mix in bread crumbs, butter, parsley, and lemon zest. Season with sea salt.

Mound 1 teaspoon (5 ml) chorizo over each clam.

Place the clams close together on the bottom grill rack. Wrap the top grill rack in heavy-duty aluminum foil, place the rack on the outside rim of the grill (an inch or two above the clams), and poke about 15 holes in the foil with a paring knife, above the clams.

Fill a chimney starter halfway with charcoal briquettes and light them. When they are very hot (you cannot hold your hand over the fire for more than 5 seconds), use tongs to grab the hot coals one by one and place on aluminum-lined rack in an even layer (A).

Broil clams for 4 to 6 minutes, until juices start to bubble.

This next step is a two-person job: Wearing heat-proof gloves, one person should remove the foil-covered rack. The other person can sprinkle the bacon topping over the clams. Replace the top rack and broil clams 3 to 5 minutes more, until the topping starts to brown (B).

Serve hot, with lemon wedges and Tabasco sauce.

YIELD: 4 appetizer servings

★ POT LIKKER AND ★ CORNMEAL DUMPLINGS

1 batch pot likker from Andy's Famous Collards (page 147)

½ cup (70 g) cornmeal

½ cup (62.5 g) flour

1 teaspoon (4.6 g) baking powder

½ teaspoon (3 g) kosher salt

2 tablespoons (28 g) cold unsalted butter, cut into 8 pieces

¼ cup (37.5 g) chopped Tasso ham

1 scallion, cut into ½-inch (1.3-cm) pieces

1 egg white

½ cup (120 ml) buttermilk

½ teaspoon (2.5 ml) Tabasco sauce

Back in the slave days, it was fashionable to overcook vegetables almost to mush. Owners would discard the liquid, but the slaves, who were the ones actually doing the cooking, were smart and knew this was where all the nutrients were—not to mention flavor. They saved the liquid, which became known as "pot likker." We like to use the "likker" from our collards and make a full-on appetizer of it with cornmeal dumplings.

In a large saucepan, bring pot likker to a simmer over medium heat. Reduce heat to low and continue simmering.

In the bowl of a food processor fitted with the steel blade, combine the cornmeal, flour, baking powder, and salt. Pulse for 10 seconds to blend. Add the butter, Tasso ham, and scallion, and pulse until mixture is crumbly. Transfer to a mixing bowl.

In a second bowl, beat the egg white lightly with a fork. Add the buttermilk and Tabasco sauce, and mix well. Make a well in the center of the dry ingredients and pour the buttermilk mixture in. Blend the ingredients to form a soft dough. Allow dough to rest for 5 minutes.

Using a small scoop or wet hands, form the dough into balls about the size of a quarter, dropping them into the simmering "likker" as you go. You should have 24 dumplings, which should cover the surface of the simmering liquid but barely touch each other. (If necessary, cook the dumplings in two batches.) Cover the pot with a tight-fitting lid and simmer gently, without peeking, for 15 minutes.

The dumplings should look puffed, smooth, and almost dry on top, and the centers should be cooked through. If not, cover and simmer for 5 minutes more. Ladle the pot likker into 6 shallow bowls and serve each with 4 dumplings on top.

YIELD: 6 servings

PORK BUTT, BY ANY OTHER NAME...

TASSO HAM, WHICH GIVES THE DUMPLINGS INCREDIBLE FLAVOR, IS KNOWN AS THE PRIDE OF LOUISIANA. HAM IS REALLY A MISNOMER, BECAUSE IN FACT IT IS A CREOLE- SPICED SMOKED PORK BUTT.

★ TENDER KENTUCKY-STYLE ★ LAMB SHANKS WITH TANGY MUTTON DIP

6 lamb shanks, about 12 ounces (340 g) each

¼ cup (72 g) kosher salt

¼ cup (24 g) coarsely ground black pepper

1 tablespoon (9 g) garlic powder

1 tablespoon (6.9 g) onion powder

2 teaspoons (3.6 g) cayenne pepper

2 cups (475 ml) Tangy Mutton Dip (recipe follows)

12 ounces (355 ml) American lager

Farmworkers, slaves, and cowboys on the trail were often left with throwaway meats—gnarly, tough-to-cook cuts like the shoulder, short rib, or shank that the farm owners had no interest in. Often, these cuts were spoiled (thus the invention of vinegar-based sauces or "dips" to cover up the off-flavors). It was discovered, though, that slowly roasting these meats by a campfire produced something magical. We'll take the shoulder over the tenderloin any day!

We look to Kentucky and the local tradition of cooking whole mutton for our inspiration in this dish. Mutton is a mature lamb—what most of us know as a sheep. And it's a perfect example of using the barbecue method to transform a tough, gamey, generally undesirable protein into something extraordinary. We like to use lamb shank, but you could substitute lamb shoulder or even a piece of mutton shoulder if you can find it.

On a large cutting board, trim excess fat and silver skin off shanks. Transfer to a platter or sheet pan, and set aside.

Mix salt, pepper, garlic powder, onion powder, and cayenne together in a small bowl. Sprinkle over lamb shanks, cover, and refrigerate for 1 hour.

While shanks are in the refrigerator, prepare smoker and bring temperature to 250°F (121°C). We recommend an assertive wood, like oak or hickory, for these babies.

Remove the shanks from the refrigerator and smoke for 2 hours.

Transfer the shanks to a disposable aluminum pan and pour 1 cup (235 ml) mutton dip and the beer over the meat. Cover pan tightly with foil and cook on the smoker for 1 to 2 hours, or until meat is meltingly tender. To test, pick up a shank with a fork. If the meat pulls away from the bone, congratulations! You have meltingly tender lamb.

To serve, strategically place a bowl of the remaining 1 cup (235 ml) mutton dip (which you have warmed) near a platter of the shanks. Encourage your guests to pull the meat from the bones with their hands and dip into the flavorful mutton dip. Do you think farmworkers or cowboys worried about silverware or napkins?

YIELD: 6 servings

TANGY MUTTON DIP

1 cup (235 ml) water

1 cup (235 ml) Worcestershire sauce

½ cup (120 g) packed brown sugar

¼ cup (60 g) yellow mustard

1 tablespoon (6.9 g) onion powder

1 tablespoon (9 g) garlic powder

2 teaspoons (10 ml) chipotle hot sauce

Kosher salt and freshly cracked black pepper, to taste

In a small saucepan over medium heat, bring all ingredients to a light boil. Reduce heat to low and simmer for 30 minutes. Remove from heat and cool. Serve with Tender Kentucky-Style Lamb Shanks.

YIELD: 2 cups (475 ml)

★ JERK CHICKEN, FLOWERPOT STYLE ★

FOR JERK MARINADE:

2 tablespoons (30 ml) white vinegar

1 tablespoon (15 ml) molasses

1 tablespoon (15 g) brown sugar

1 tablespoon (6 g) freshly ground black pepper

1 habanero pepper, stem and seeds removed (use gloves)

2 teaspoons (12 g) kosher salt

1 teaspoon (2.3 g) ground cinnamon

½ teaspoon (1.3 g) toasted, ground cumin seeds

½ teaspoon (0.7 g) dried thyme

½ teaspoon (0.7 g) dried oregano

½ teaspoon (1 g) ground allspice

¼ teaspoon (0.6 g) ground nutmeg

FOR CHICKEN:

1 whole chicken (2½ to 3 pounds, or 1 kg to 1.37 kg), cut in half, backbone removed

1 lime, cut into 6 wedges

2 teaspoons (12 g) sea salt, or to taste

Papaya Salad (recipe follows)

SPECIAL EQUIPMENT:

12- to 14-inch (30- to 35-cm) terra-cotta flowerpot with bottom saucer, and enough sand to fill the pot halfway; 4 metal skewers (16 inches, or 40 cm); chimney starter; charcoal briquettes (not lump charcoal)

Just for fun, one day we were researching different ways to make grills. We saw some different do-it-yourself ideas on TV, and we loved this flowerpot method. This dish is a tribute to our friend Gary Ferguson, who lives in Kingston, Jamaica. Gary became an honorary member of our IQUE team after spending four rainy days with us in Vermont during a Harpoon Championship of New England Barbecue competition. One night he treated us all to one of his local specialties, making a big dinner with amazing jerk chicken. (We've adapted it to the flowerpot; it works great on a standard grill, too.) Andy developed a papaya salad that deliciously complements the chicken.

To make the marinade: In a blender or food processor fitted with the steel blade, combine the marinade ingredients and process until smooth.

To make the chicken: Rub the marinade all over the surface of the chicken and under the skin (be careful not to tear it).

Lay one of the chicken halves skin-side up on a cutting board. Insert 2 skewers through the breast to the leg, about 1 inch (2.5 cm) apart, as close to the leg bone as possible to keep the chicken from sliding off. Repeat with the other chicken half and remaining 2 skewers. Tuck the wing tips against each breast to form triangles. Set the chicken aside while you construct the flowerpot grill.

Pour sand into the flowerpot and place the pot on the saucer.

Fill a chimney starter about halfway with charcoal briquettes. Light the briquettes and let them burn until you cannot hold your hand above the chimney starter for more than 10 seconds. Very carefully, pour coals into flowerpot, or use long-handled tongs to transfer them one by one. There should be about 20 briquettes, enough to cover the sand in a single layer.

JERK CHICKEN, FLOWERPOT STYLE (CONTINUED)

Position the chicken halves over the flowerpot, with the skewers resting on the lip of the pot. Grill, skin-side down, for 10 minutes, then turn the chicken over. After 10 more minutes, use an instant-read thermometer to check the temperature at the thickest part of each thigh—it should register 165°F (74°C). If not, add 5 more coals to the fire and continue cooking, flipping every 10 minutes, for a total of 30 to 40 minutes. When chicken is done, transfer to a cutting board and let rest for 10 minutes before removing the skewers.

To serve: Cut chicken into quarters and arrange on a serving platter. Squeeze lime wedges over chicken and sprinkle with sea salt. Pass the Papaya Salad on the side.

YIELD: 4 servings

Note: You must let the flowerpot cool completely before cleaning. Do not add water while it's hot or it will shatter.

PAPAYA SALAD

1 ripe papaya, peeled, seeded, and cut into ½-inch (1.3-cm) dice

¼ cup (60 ml) spiced rum

1 habanero pepper, stem and seeds removed, minced (wear gloves)

¾ cup (175 ml) fresh lime juice (from about 6 limes)

1 small red onion, quartered lengthwise, then thinly sliced crosswise

½ head (1 pound, or 455 g) Savoy cabbage, outer leaves removed, cored, and cut into ¼-inch (6-mm) dice

2 tablespoons (30 ml) olive oil

Kosher salt and freshly cracked black pepper, to taste

This is a great tropical salad whose flavors are a perfect counterbalance to the spicy jerk chicken. It works equally well with mango, so choose your fruit! Like jerk cooking, both fruits are indigenous to Jamaica. You may have some salad left over after your chicken dinner, but it keeps well in the refrigerator.

In a large bowl, toss the papaya, rum, habanero, lime juice, onion, cabbage, and oil. Mix well, and season to taste with salt and pepper. Refrigerate until chicken is ready and toss again before serving.

YIELD: 9 cups (2.1 L) or 4 to 8 servings

★ NEW YORK STRIP IN A FLOWERPOT ★ AND VEGGIE PACKS

2 New York strip loins (2 pounds, or 1 kg, each), fat trimmed to ¼ inch (6 mm)

Kosher salt and freshly cracked black pepper, to taste

Veggie Packs (recipe follows)

SPECIAL EQUIPMENT:

12- to 14-inch (30- to 35-cm) terra-cotta flowerpot with bottom saucer, and enough sand to fill the pot halfway; 5 metal skewers (16 inches, or 40 cm); chimney starter; charcoal briquettes (not lump charcoal)

Though the effort of constructing a grill in a flowerpot may be superfluous to those who have backyards and/or decks with a kettle grill, smoker, or both, this is a terrific solution for city dwellers or people without much space. You can set it up on a fire escape wide enough to move around, a sidewalk or driveway, or a rooftop deck (as long as it doesn't have a wood surface). It's similar to tandoori cooking, where heat rises through a clay oven.

Pour sand into the flowerpot and place the pot on the saucer.

Fill a chimney starter about halfway with charcoal briquettes. Light the briquettes and let them burn until you cannot hold your hand above the chimney starter for more than 10 seconds. Very carefully, pour coals into flowerpot, or use long-handled tongs to transfer them one by one. There should be about 20 briquettes, enough to cover the sand in a single layer.

Spear a steak with 3 of the skewers, spacing them about 1 inch (2.5 cm) apart across the width of the steak and running all the way through. Spear the second steak onto the same skewers. Season heavily with salt and pepper, lightly pressing seasoning into the meat.

A: GRILLING OVER A FLOWERPOT.

B: (CONTINUED.)

C: FLOWERPOT-GRILLED NEW YORK
STRIP STEAK.

NEW YORK STRIP IN A FLOWERPOT AND VEGGIE PACKS (CONTINUED)

Place the 2 remaining skewers across the rim of the flowerpot. Center the steak over the coals, with the skewers resting on the rim of the flowerpot (**A & B**). Roast for 10 minutes, then flip over (get out those heatproof gloves; the skewers will be hot). Cook for 10 minutes more. If steak is not done after 20 minutes total, add 6 more briquettes. Continue to cook and flip every 10 minutes until the steak temperature is 10°F (5°C) lower than your desired doneness—120°F (49°C) for rare, 130°F (54°C) for medium-rare, and 140°F (60°C) for medium. Transfer the steak to a cutting board to rest while you cook the Veggie Packs (**C**).

To serve, carve the steak across the grain into ½-inch (1.3-cm) slices. Arrange on a platter. Place the Veggie Packs on another platter and let guests serve themselves.

YIELD: 8 servings

VEGGIE PACKS

¼ cup (40 g) roughly chopped smoked bacon

1 carrot, peeled and sliced ¼ inch (6 mm) thick

1 parsnip, peeled and sliced ¼ inch (6 mm) thick

1 fennel bulb, top removed, bulb cored, and cut into ⅛-inch (3-mm) wedges

4 baby Yukon gold or new potatoes, cut into quarters

1 medium yellow onion, cut into chunks

1 clove garlic, chopped

1½ teaspoons (1.1 g) minced fresh rosemary leaves

¼ cup (15 g) roughly chopped flat-leaf Italian parsley

¼ cup (60 ml) extra-virgin olive oil

Kosher salt and freshly cracked black pepper, to taste

¼ cup (60 ml) low-sodium chicken or beef stock

SPECIAL EQUIPMENT:

Heavy-duty aluminum foil

In a large bowl, combine the bacon, carrot, parsnip, fennel, potatoes, onion, garlic, rosemary, parsley, oil, salt, and pepper, and toss until evenly coated with the oil. Season with additional salt and pepper if desired.

Tear off 2 sheets of aluminum foil, each about 1½ feet (45 cm) long, and lay them out on a work surface. Divide the vegetables evenly between the sheets, and gather the sides of the foil up to make loose, open pouches. Spoon about 2 tablespoons (30 ml) of stock into each pouch and close them up tightly, forming a good seal to prevent leakage.

While the steak is resting, arrange the packs in the coals and cook for 10 minutes. Flip the packs over, and cook for 10 minutes more. Slide a paring knife into the vegetables. They are done when it slides in easily. Carefully remove from flowerpot (beware of the hot stock), and let cool for 2 minutes before opening the packs.

YIELD: 8 servings

Note: You must let the flowerpot cool completely before cleaning. Do not add water while it's hot or it will shatter.

★ TANDOORI SHRIMP IN A FLOWERPOT ★

FOR MARINADE:

½ cup (8 g) packed fresh cilantro sprigs

2 teaspoons (6 g) kosher salt

1-inch (2.5-cm) piece fresh ginger, peeled

1 clove garlic, peeled

1 cup (235 ml) yogurt

1 lime, juiced, and zest removed with a vegetable peeler and minced

1 tablespoon (7.5 g) garam masala

2 teaspoons (4 g) freshly ground black pepper

1 teaspoon (4 g) ground annatto seed

1 teaspoon (1.8 g) cayenne pepper

FOR SKEWERS:

1 pound (455 g, or about 16) cocktail shrimp, peeled and deveined, with tails on

1 slender zucchini, stem removed, cut into ½-inch (1.3-cm) rounds

½ small red onion, quartered through the stem ends

Spicy Tamarind Sauce (recipe follows)

Coconut Basmati Rice (recipe follows)

SPECIAL EQUIPMENT:

12- to 14-inch (30- to 35-cm) terra-cotta flowerpot with bottom saucer, and enough sand to fill the pot halfway; 4 metal skewers (16 inches, or 40 cm); chimney starter; charcoal briquettes (not lump charcoal)

This cooking method is so much like a tandoori oven that we thought we would be remiss not having a tandoori dish. With the Coconut Basmati Rice and Spicy Tamarind Sauce, this is a delicious meal, but the shrimp also make great appetizers.

To make the marinade: In a food processor fitted with a steel blade, combine the cilantro, salt, ginger, and garlic and pulse until finely chopped. Add yogurt, lime juice and zest, garam masala, pepper, ground annatto, and cayenne, and process until well blended. Reserve.

To make the skewers: Thread the shrimp, zucchini, and onion sections alternately onto the skewers. The ingredients should be centered on the skewers, touching but not squished together, with a few inches of empty space at both ends for proper cooking.

Place the skewers on a large plate or baking pan and pour the marinade over them. Marinate for 2 to 4 hours, rotating every 30 minutes.

While the skewers are marinating, assemble the grill:

Follow directions for flowerpot grill on page 155, but let briquettes in the chimney starter burn until you cannot hold your hand above them for more than 3 to 4 seconds.

One at a time, lift the skewers out of the marinade, tapping the ends to knock off any excess marinade. Center the skewers over the coals, with the skewers resting on the lip of the flower pot, and roast for 3 to 4 minutes per side for a total of 6 to 8 minutes. Remove shrimp and vegetables from the skewers and serve with Spicy Tamarind Sauce and Coconut Basmati Rice on the side.

YIELD: 4 to 6 side dish or 2 to 3 main course servings

SPICY TAMARIND SAUCE

1 tablespoon (15 ml) vegetable oil

¼ cup (32.5 g) chopped fresh ginger

1 teaspoon (2.5 g) toasted, ground cumin seeds

½ teaspoon (1.3 g) garam masala

½ teaspoon (0.6 g) crushed red pepper flakes

½ teaspoon (1 g) fennel seeds

2 cups (475 ml) water

1 cup (225 g) packed light brown sugar

⅓ cup (80 ml) red wine vinegar

¼ cup (115 g) tamarind from a block of seedless pulp (add a little more if the block has seeds)

¼ cup (4 g) chopped fresh cilantro

Tamarind generally comes in bars with the seeds still in it. You can buy the paste, but we like the bars better.

In a saucepan over medium heat, heat the oil. Add the ginger, cumin, garam masala, red pepper, and fennel. Fry for about 2 minutes or until fragrant, stirring and scraping the pan constantly. Add the water, stirring to scrape up any seasoning stuck to the pan, and then the brown sugar, vinegar, and tamarind. Bring to a boil, stirring to break up and dissolve the tamarind pulp as much as possible. Adjust the heat to a simmer and cook, stirring often, until the mixture turns syrupy, about 30 minutes. (It should be just thick enough to coat the back of a metal spoon at this point. The sauce will continue to thicken as it cools.)

Strain sauce into a heat-proof bowl, pressing and scraping as much tamarind pulp through the strainer as possible. Stir in the cilantro, and let cool to room temperature before using.

The sauce will keep, refrigerated, for 1 to 2 weeks.

YIELD: 1 cup (235 ml)

COCONUT BASMATI RICE

1 tablespoon (15 ml) vegetable oil

2 cloves garlic, minced

One 14-ounce (425-ml) can unsweetened coconut milk

1¼ cups (285 ml) water

1 tablespoon (6.3 g) curry powder

1½ cups (292.5 g) uncooked basmati rice

½ cup (75 g) golden raisins

Kosher salt and freshly cracked black pepper, to taste, plus 1 teaspoon (6 g) salt

In a heavy-bottomed 2-quart (1.9-L) saucepan over medium heat, combine the oil and garlic and cook, stirring frequently, until garlic is fragrant and golden, 3 to 4 minutes. Stir in the coconut milk, water, and curry powder, mixing well, and bring to a boil.

Add the rice, raisins, and 1 teaspoon (6 g) salt, stir well, and return to a boil. Reduce heat to low, cover the pan, and simmer gently for 5 minutes. Stir again, scraping the bottom of the pan to prevent sticking. Cover the pan and continue to cook gently until the rice is tender but not mushy, 12 to 15 minutes more. Adjust seasoning with salt and pepper.

Fluff the rice with a fork, and pile onto a serving platter.

YIELD: 6 cups (990 g)

IQUE
BBQ COOKING TEAM
BOSTON • HOPKINTON • NEW YORK • CAPE COD • AUSTRALIA • VERMONT
2009 GRAND CHAMPION
JACK DANIELS WORLD CHAMPIONSHIP INVITATIONAL BARBEQUE CONTE

★ CHAPTER 6 ★

WAIT 'TIL YOU TRY THIS

(UNBELIEVABLE RESULTS THAT TAKE TIME)

RESERVE CHAMPION
I LOVE BARBECUE FESTIVAL
LAKE PLACID, NEW YORK

CREATING GREAT BARBECUE takes a lot of patience. Many fantastic recipes don't require all that much active preparation time, but necessitate hours of sitting, tending the fire, and monitoring smoking temperature. (That's what beer is for.) The recipes in this chapter take even more patience—sometimes several days' worth—and planning. But we promise you, they are worth every single second that you spend, and wait.

In the days before modern storage and refrigeration, people utilized various methods for preserving meat and vegetables, from salt cures to brines to pickling to smoking. The following recipes take advantage of all of these. Though we no longer need them to preserve the food, it turns out these processes, in their own ways, impart so much flavor and texture that we think they're well worth the time. We cure both duck and pork belly, yielding two completely different results—both of which can then be eaten on their own or built on to create other spectacular dishes, as we do in a po' boy sandwich with smoked duck confit and in the Six-Day Bacon of the Gods. Six-Day Bacon of the Gods is made using a traditional curing technique, but the brine and spices we apply make it anything but ordinary. Combining it with Three-Day BBQ Kimchi (you guessed it—another preserving method) takes it to another level altogether.

Feel free to use any of the stand-alone recipes in this chapter on their own. Mix and match them as the mood strikes you, with other recipes in the book, or as we've suggested in our extravagant combinations of classic techniques.

★ SIX-DAY BACON OF THE GODS ★

FOR MARINADE:

10 cups (2.4 L) water

1 cup (200 g) salt

2 cups (450 g) packed light brown sugar

1 cup (235 ml) molasses

1 green bell pepper, cored, seeded, and roughly chopped

2 ribs celery, cut into ¼-inch (6-mm) dice

1 medium yellow onion, chopped

1 bay leaf

2 teaspoons (2.8 g) dried thyme

2 pounds (1 kg) pork belly, skin on, cut into 8 square pieces (2 ounces, or 55 g each)

FOR SLURRY:

½ cup (120 ml) white vinegar

½ cup (120 ml) cayenne pepper sauce, such as Frank's Red Hot Sauce

1 cup (200 g) salt

Vegetable oil, for frying

Three-Day BBQ Kimchi (recipe follows)

SPECIAL EQUIPMENT:

Bamboo or wood steamer, wok, deep fryer or deep sauté pan

When IQUE teammate Ed Doyle and I (Andy) were traveling in Thailand, we stumbled on a weekend market. Of everything we tasted there, it was the bacon we couldn't get out of our minds, and we spent the next three days talking about how to make it. There is now a version on the menu at Tremont 647.

For this book, Chris and I talked about blending flavors of the southern United States with eastern influences and came up with this bacon, which has it all—salt, "candy" (in the form of caramelized belly fat), and spice. It's guaranteed to leave you and your guests swooning. If that's not a worthwhile payoff, we don't know what is.

To make the marinade: In a large saucepan over high heat, bring the marinade ingredients to a boil. Remove from heat and cool liquid until it registers 42°F (5°C) or lower.

Place the pork belly in a 9 × 13-inch (23 × 33-cm) pan, pour marinade over the belly, cover, and refrigerate for 3 days.

Prepare smoker and bring temperature to 225°F (107°C). Place pork belly on the grate and smoke for 30 minutes.

While the pork is smoking, fill a wok with 3 inches (7.5 cm) of water, set a bamboo or wooden steamer inside, and spray the inside with nonstick spray. Also, set a cooling rack into a sheet pan.

Remove the pork from the smoker, place it skin-side up in the steamer, and steam it over low heat for 2 to 2½ hours (checking and adding water as needed), until the skin is translucent. Remove from steamer and place on the prepared cooling rack until it is cool to the touch. Pierce all sides with a fork.

To make the slurry: In a small bowl, mix the vinegar, hot sauce, and salt.

When the pork belly has cooled, rub slurry liberally all over. Cover and refrigerate for 3 days. After 3 days, wipe slurry off.

Fill a deep fryer or a deep sauté pan with enough oil to cover the pork and bring it to 350°F (180°C) over high heat. Fry the pork belly for 2 to 4 minutes, until it is golden brown and the skin is blistering. Transfer to a cutting board and blot dry with paper towels.

To serve, use a very sharp knife to slice downward through the skin, making ¼- to ½-inch (6-mm to 1.3-cm) slices. Layer the pork belly on Buttermilk Slider Rolls (page 71) or Asian-style steamed buns, with Three-Day BBQ Kimchi on top.

YIELD: 8 appetizer servings

THREE-DAY BBQ KIMCHI

1 head celery root (also known as celeriac), peeled and shredded

1 cup (70 g) shredded green cabbage

1 red onion, julienned

1 green bell pepper, cored, seeded, and julienned

½ bunch parsley, leaves only, roughly chopped

2 cloves garlic, minced

2 tablespoons (30 ml) IQUE BBQ Sauce (page 35), or Bill Arnold's Blues Hog Sauce (see Resources, page 218)

2 tablespoons (32 g) chili garlic paste

3 tablespoons (45 g) kosher salt

1 to 2 cups (235 to 475 ml) water, optional

In a large bowl, mix the celery root, cabbage, onion, bell pepper, parsley, garlic, BBQ sauce, chili garlic paste, and salt and stir to combine. Transfer to a tall, cylindrical container. Place a weight, such as several small plates, on top of the vegetables, and let sit for 1 hour so the natural juices rise up and cover the vegetables. If the mixture does not yield enough natural juices, add water just to cover vegetables.

Cover the container tightly with plastic wrap. Store in a basement or another cool, dark, dry place for 3 days. Every evening, poke a few holes in the plastic wrap to ventilate it overnight, and every morning add another layer of plastic wrap to seal it during the day.

On the third day, transfer the kimchi to the refrigerator. It will keep for up to 10 days.

YIELD: 3 cups (710 ml)

★ DUCK, DUCK, SMOKE ★

We'll admit it. When planning our annual trip to New Orleans Jazz Fest we look at the food vendor lineup before the musicians. Our festival plan revolves around sampling as much fried chicken, jambalaya, po' boys, boudin balls, and crawfish pie as possible.

Here is our ode to high-end festival food, in which we use whole ducks to create a very special po' boy sandwich. The legs are used to make a confit, which, traditionally, is made by curing the legs and then slow-cooking them in fat. In this recipe, in addition to the cure, we smoke the legs. The breast meat is prepared in the style of pastrami. Two classic duck preparations with, of course, smoke added to the mix. Both the confit and the pastrami are nice stand-alone recipes with many uses. The confit is a great addition to the Campfire Cassoulet (page 183). You could also serve the pastrami in a sandwich with spicy mustard, or as an accompaniment to a mixed greens and fruit salad.

For the confit and pastrami, you will have to butcher and smoke two ducks (see sidebar, page 174). The confit needs a week of refrigeration, and brining the pastrami is a two-day process, so plan accordingly. (See sidebar, page 176 for recommended step-by-step preparation.)

DUCK, DUCK, SMOKE PO' BOY

1 recipe Smoked Duck Confit (recipe follows)

Duck Cracklin's (recipe follows)

4 breasts Duck Pastrami (recipe follows)

12-inch (30-cm) loaf French-style bread

¾ cup (175 ml) spicy mustard (we recommend Zatarain's Creole Mustard)

2 cups (475 ml) Braised Red Cabbage, at room temperature (recipe follows)

Both Duck Confit and Duck Pastrami are very versatile ingredients to have stashed in the refrigerator. But they also form the basis for this mind-blowing po' boy–style sandwich.

Preheat oven to 375°F (190°C, or gas mark 5).

Place the baking dish with the Smoked Duck Confit in the oven just until the fat melts. Spread the cracklin's (A) out on a sheet pan and place in oven until crisp, about 10 minutes.

Meanwhile, take the pastrami from the refrigerator and slice thinly with a sharp knife (B & C). Let sit until it comes to room temperature.

A: MAKING DUCK CRACKLIN'S (SMOKED DUCK CONFIT IN BACKGROUND).

B: SLICING DUCK PASTRAMI . . .

C: . . . AND THE RESULT.

DUCK, DUCK, SMOKE PO' BOY (CONTINUED)

Remove the baking dish from the oven. One at a time, with a slotted spoon, lift the legs and garlic out of the baking dish, letting any excess fat drip off, and transfer legs to a straight-sided sauté pan filled with 1 inch (2.5 cm) of duck fat from the confit. Set garlic aside. Over medium heat, crisp the legs, skin-side down, for 3 to 5 minutes, until skin is golden brown. Remove legs from the pan and place on a paper towel until cool enough to touch. Using your hands, shred the meat and crispy skin. Discard the bones.

Slip the roasted garlic cloves out of their skins and mash into a smooth paste with a fork.

Strain the remaining duck fat from the confit (**D**) through cheesecloth, and refrigerate for up to 2 weeks or freeze for up to 2 months. Be sure to save this fat for BBQ Gravy Fries (page 116) or something equally delectable.

To assemble the po' boy, slice the French bread lengthwise. Smear the roasted garlic paste on the top piece of bread. Layer the pulled confit on first, then stack the sliced pastrami on top. Drizzle with mustard, and pile Braised Red Cabbage over all. Sprinkle with the cracklin's. You can add a dollop of 647 Secret Sauce (page 70) to send the sandwich in a Reuben direction (**E**).

With a serrated knife, slice the sandwich crosswise into 6 pieces. Use 6-inch (15-cm) bamboo skewers to hold each sandwich together and serve immediately.

YIELD: 6 servings

DUCK PASTRAMI

Duck Pastrami Brine (recipe follows)

4 boneless duck breasts, all fat and skin intact (from two 4-pound, or 2-kg, ducks)

Duck Pastrami Rub (recipe follows)

Place chilled Pastrami Brine in a 2-quart (1.9-L) container and submerge the duck breasts. Refrigerate for 48 hours.

Remove breasts from the brine and rinse them, shaking off excess water. Coat the breasts with Pastrami Rub on both sides, pressing gently to help it adhere to the skin.

Prepare smoker and bring temperature to 225°F (107°C), using a fruit wood for flavor. Smoke the duck breasts, skin-side down, for 1½ hours. Cool cooked breasts to room temperature, wrap tightly in plastic wrap, and refrigerate until you are ready to assemble the sandwiches (up to 1 week).

YIELD: 6 servings

D: SMOKED DUCK CONFIT

E: DUCK, DUCK, SMOKE PO' BOY—TRULY WORTH THE TIME AND EFFORT

DUCK PASTRAMI BRINE

3 cups (710 ml) water

⅓ cup (100 g) kosher salt

¼ cup (37.5 g) packed brown sugar

¼ cup (25 g) coarsely ground black pepper

1 tablespoon (9 g) garlic powder

2 bay leaves

Place all ingredients in a medium saucepan and bring to a boil. Remove from heat and stir to dissolve salt and sugar completely. Let cool to room temperature and refrigerate until cold.

YIELD: About 1 quart (946 ml)

DUCK PASTRAMI RUB

¼ cup (25 g) coarsely ground black pepper

¼ cup (25 g) coarsely ground coriander seeds

2 tablespoons (15 g) chili powder

2 tablespoons (18 g) garlic powder

In a mixing bowl, combine all ingredients. Will keep, covered, for 1 month.

YIELD: ¾ cup (170 g)

TO BUTCHER A DUCK (OR TWO)

PLACE THE DUCK ON A CUTTING BOARD BREAST-SIDE UP. WITH A SHARP KNIFE, REMOVE WINGS. CUT ALONG BOTH SIDES OF THE BREAST BONE AND AGAINST RIB CAGE TO REMOVE BREASTS, LEAVING THE SKIN ON. RESERVE THE BREASTS FOR THE DUCK PASTRAMI. REMOVE THE LEG QUARTERS, LEAVING THE SKIN ON, AND RESERVE FOR THE DUCK CONFIT. TRIM ALL OF THE FAT AND SKIN FROM THE CARCASS, AND CUT INTO SMALL PIECES. RESERVE THE FAT AND THE SKIN TO MAKE CRACKLIN'S AND RENDERED DUCK FAT. COVER AND REFRIGERATE THE RESERVED DUCK PARTS UNTIL READY TO USE. FREEZE THE WINGS AND TRIMMED CARCASS FOR STOCK.

SMOKED DUCK CONFIT

FOR CONFIT CURE:

3 tablespoons (54 g) kosher salt

¼ cup (15 g) minced parsley

1 tablespoon (6 g) minced lemon zest

1 tablespoon (7.5 g) chili powder

1 teaspoon (2.4 g) onion powder

1 teaspoon (3 g) garlic powder

4 duck legs (from two 4-pound, or 2-kg, ducks)

Rendered fat from making the Duck Cracklin's
(page 177)

2 heads garlic, cut in half lengthwise,
excess papery skin discarded

Olive oil, as needed

To make the confit cure: In a bowl, combine the salt, parsley, zest, chili powder, onion powder, and garlic powder and mix well.

Place the duck legs in a shallow baking dish and coat them on both sides with the cure. Cover and refrigerate for 24 hours.

While the legs are curing, make the Duck Cracklin's (page 177).

After 24 hours, remove the legs from the refrigerator and rinse off the cure.

Prepare smoker and bring temperature to 225°F (107°C), using a fruit wood for flavor. Smoke the duck legs for 1 hour.

In a medium saucepan over medium-low heat, melt the duck fat.

Remove the legs from the smoker. Place a high-sided baking dish or disposable aluminum pan on the smoker grate. Put the legs and garlic halves in the pan, then pour the melted fat over them. If the fat does not completely cover the legs, use some inexpensive olive oil to cover. Cook, uncovered, for 3 to 4 hours, or until the meat is easily pulled from the bone. If you prefer, you can do this step in your oven.

Remove the pan from the smoker and let cool to room temperature. Cover and refrigerate, making sure legs and garlic are completely submerged in the fat, for 1 week.

YIELD: 6 servings

TIME MANAGEMENT WITH DUCKS

WE WARNED YOU THAT THE RECIPES IN THIS CHAPTER WEREN'T FOR ANYBODY WHO DEMANDS INSTANT GRATIFICATION. BUT WE RECOGNIZE THAT THIS PARTICULAR ONE MIGHT STRAIN THE PATIENCE OF EVEN THE MOST DEDICATED AMONG YOU. IT WAS IMPORTANT TO US TO USE EVERY PART OF THE DUCK, BOTH FOR THE MIND-BLOWING SANDWICHES AND BECAUSE EVERY BIT IS SO DELICIOUS WE COULDN'T BEAR TO WASTE A DROP. WE'VE WRITTEN THE RECIPE IN THE ORDER WE THINK MAKES THE MOST SENSE TO GET TO YOUR OWN DUCK, DUCK, SMOKE PO' BOYS, BUT FOR A LITTLE EXTRA HELP, HERE'S OUR AT-A-GLANCE LIST OF THE STEPS IN THE ORDER THAT MAKE THE MOST SENSE TO US. ENJOY!

DAY 1:

MAKE PASTRAMI BRINE AND CONFIT CURE.

REMOVE BREASTS FROM BOTH DUCKS.

PLACE BREASTS IN BRINE.

REMOVE LEGS FROM BOTH DUCKS, KEEPING SKIN INTACT.

APPLY CONFIT CURE TO THE LEGS.

TRIM DUCK CARCASSES OF ALL FAT AND MAKE THE CRACKLIN'S.

DAY 2: (24 HOURS LATER)

RINSE CURE FROM THE LEGS AND RETURN TO REFRIGERATOR.

DAY 3: (48 HOURS LATER)

MAKE THE PASTRAMI RUB.

REMOVE BREASTS FROM BRINE, PAT DRY. RUB WITH PASTRAMI RUB.

SMOKE BREASTS AND LEGS.

STORE THE PASTRAMI AND CONFIT ACCORDING TO INSTRUCTIONS IN THE RECIPE.

DAY 4: (1 WEEK LATER)

ASSEMBLE THE SANDWICHES ACCORDING TO INSTRUCTIONS IN THE RECIPE.

DUCK CRACKLIN'S

Reserved skin and fat from two
4-pound (2-kg) ducks

1 cup (235 ml) water

Place the pieces of duck skin and fat in a heavy-bottomed, 3-quart (2.8-L) saucepan with the water and simmer, uncovered, over medium-low heat until all of the duck skin has rendered into very crispy pieces, 3 to 5 hours. Stir occasionally throughout the cooking process, scraping the bottom of the pan to prevent sticking. Watch the cracklin's closely toward the end of cooking to prevent overbrowning; they should be crisp and light golden brown. Remove the browned cracklin's from the fat with a slotted spoon, spread on a paper towel–lined plate to drain, and let cool to room temperature. Refrigerate in a resealable plastic bag until ready to use. Strain the duck fat through cheesecloth and refrigerate. Use the duck fat in the Smoked Duck Confit (page 175).

YIELD: 6 servings

BRAISED RED CABBAGE

4 tablespoons (½ stick, or 55 g) unsalted butter, divided

1 small yellow onion, thinly sliced

½ cup (115 g) packed brown sugar

½ cup (120 ml) cider vinegar

¼ cup (60 ml) water

1½ pounds (680 g) red cabbage, cored and shredded to make 10 cups (2.4 L)

Kosher salt and freshly cracked black pepper, to taste

In a large sauté pan over medium heat, melt 2 tablespoons (28 g) of the butter. Add onion and sauté until soft and just beginning to brown. Stir in the sugar, vinegar, water, and remaining 2 tablespoons (28 g) butter, then add the cabbage. Raise heat to medium-high and bring to a boil. Adjust heat so the cabbage simmers gently for 1 hour, stirring and folding with tongs occasionally. Season with salt and pepper.

Let cool to room temperature. If not using the cabbage immediately to make the po' boys, cover and refrigerate for up to 1 week.

YIELD: 3 cups (710 ml)

★ JAMIE'S PIG EAR TERRINE ★

FOR LIME SIMPLE SYRUP:

½ cup (120 ml) water

⅔ cup (132 g) sugar

½ cup (120 ml) fresh lime juice
(from about 4 limes)

18 to 20 pig ears, flaps only

1 tablespoon (18 g) kosher salt

FOR SACHET:

1 cup (60 g) packed parsley sprigs

2 ribs celery, roughly chopped

1 green bell pepper, core and seeds removed,
roughly chopped

2 dried ancho chiles, stems and seeds removed,
torn into small pieces (wear gloves)

4 cloves garlic, peeled

1 tablespoon (7 g) paprika

1 tablespoon (7.5 g) chili powder

Jamie Bissonnette, of Coppa and Toro in Boston, is one of the most wicked chefs we know. His complex flavors and mastery of offal have garnered him a reputation that extends well beyond the city. Jamie's pig ear terrine has been a favorite at Coppa since the wildly popular enoteca opened. He was generous enough to let us use his recipe, which we adapted slightly to our barbecue sensibility, using spices from some of our favorite pork dishes in the sachet.

To make the lime simple syrup: In a small saucepan set over medium heat, bring the water, sugar, and lime juice to a simmer, stirring constantly, just until sugar dissolves. Simmer gently for 5 minutes, and set aside. (You'll need 1 cup [235 ml] for the terrine; save any remaining lime syrup for another use.)

Clean the ears of any hair, and arrange them in the roasting pan with at least ½ inch (1.3 cm) of space at the top. Leave room to tuck the sachet in the middle of the pan. Season the ears with the salt.

To make the sachet: Spread out a piece of cheesecloth and fold it in half to make a 12-inch (30-cm) square. Place the parsley, celery, green pepper, ancho chiles, garlic, paprika, and chili powder in the center. Tie up the sachet with kitchen string, and tuck it in the middle of the ears in the roasting pan.

To make the terrine: Preheat oven to 200°F (93°C, or gas mark ½).

In a stockpot over medium-high heat, bring the stock, bourbon, soy sauce, sherry, brown sugar, and lime simple syrup to a simmer, stirring to dissolve sugar. Pour enough of the hot liquid over the ears to cover them by ½ inch (1.3 cm). Cover the pan tightly with plastic wrap, then with aluminum foil, and place in the oven until the ears are very tender, about

FOR TERRINE:

3 quarts (2.8 L) low-sodium chicken stock

3 cups (710 ml) bourbon

2 cups (475 ml) soy sauce

1 cup (235 ml) dry sherry

½ cup (115 g) packed light brown sugar

1 cup (235 ml) lime simple syrup

Fleur de Sel

Snipped chives

Yuzu Aioli, optional (recipe follows)

SPECIAL EQUIPMENT:

12 × 24-inch (30 × 60-cm) piece of cheesecloth; kitchen string; 18-inch-wide (45-cm) rolls of aluminum foil and plastic wrap; extra-large roasting pan (or 2 heavy-duty aluminum foil steam pans, approximately 20 × 13 inches [50 × 33 cm] and 3⅜ inches [8.75 cm] deep, stacked together); 2- to 3-quart (1.9- to 2.8-L) terrine mold, ideally 12 × 6 inches (30 × 15 cm); 2-pound (1-kg) weight, such as a brick wrapped in foil

36 hours. Lift the foil occasionally to make sure the liquid is not boiling; lower the heat slightly if it is.

After 36 hours, peel back the plastic wrap and check the ears. They should break apart easily, but not shred, and the cartilage should be just past al dente.

Cool the ears in their liquid to room temperature, then strain the liquid into a large saucepan. Discard the sachet, and boil the liquid until reduced by one-third.

While the liquid is reducing, line the terrine mold with plastic wrap, with at least a 2-inch (5-cm) overhang all around. Layer the ears snugly in the mold, leaving ⅛ inch (3 mm) of space at the top. Pour the hot liquid over the ears (you will not need it all). Shake the mold gently, then add a little more liquid if necessary to completely submerge the ears. Fold plastic wrap over the top to seal, wrap the entire terrine in a second layer of plastic wrap, and place it in a foil pan. Place a 2-pound (1-kg) weight on top and refrigerate overnight. (The weight may cause the terrine to leak, and the pan will catch the drippings.)

To unmold, peel back the plastic wrap to expose the surface of the terrine. Place a rimmed serving platter, or a cutting board with a well, over the pan and invert. Pull gently on the plastic wrap to release the terrine onto the platter, then discard the plastic.

With a hot, wet knife, slice the terrine as thinly as possible, ¼- to ½-inch (6-mm to 1.3-cm) thick. Wipe off and re-wet the knife between slices. Use a cake lifter to transfer the slices to individual serving plates, garnish with fleur de sel and chives, and serve immediately.

We like to serve the terrine with Yuzu Aioli, though any creamy and sour sauce would pair fine.

Keep the terrine refrigerated at all times, wrapped tightly in plastic. It will keep for up to 10 days.

YIELD: One 10-inch (25-cm) terrine, 20 appetizer servings

YUZU AIOLI

4 cloves garlic, minced

2 egg yolks

15 cilantro leaves, minced

½ teaspoon (0.6 g) dried red pepper flakes

1 tablespoon (15 ml) yuzu juice

1 teaspoon (5 ml) soy sauce

1 cup (235 ml) extra-virgin olive oil

Kosher salt and freshly cracked black pepper, to taste

Yuzu, a Japanese citrus, is one of our favorite fruits for sauces. The flavor is very floral, with hints of coriander. It's kind of like a cross between a Mandarin orange and a clementine. It is perhaps not the easiest to find (try Asian markets or online), and it can be expensive. If you can't find yuzu, you can use a 50/50 mix of fresh lime and fresh orange juice. But it won't be quite as good.

Place the garlic, egg yolks, cilantro, red pepper flakes, yuzu, and soy sauce in the bowl of a food processor, and pulse several times to combine. With the machine running, slowly stream in olive oil to emulsify. Season with salt and pepper. Transfer to a bowl, cover, and refrigerate until ready to use.

YIELD: 1⅓ cups (315 ml)

★ CAMPFIRE CASSOULET ★

1½ pounds (680 g) dried white beans
(cannellini or Great Northern)

2 fresh pork shanks

¼ pound (115 g) slab bacon

2 pounds (1 kg) pork rib tips

2½ pounds (1.14 kg) sweet Italian pork sausage,
casings removed, meat formed into a fatty
(see sidebar, page 185)

FOR GARLIC PEPPER DRY RUB:

¼ cup (75 g) kosher salt

¼ cup (25 g) black pepper, coarsely ground

¼ cup (25 g) garlic granules or garlic powder

This is a great dish to use up the leftover trimmings from The Ribs That Won the Jack Daniel's World Championship (page 29) or Smoked Duck Confit (page 175), but if you don't have any leftovers, it's worth starting from scratch. It's a two-day process, so it takes a little patience. But you'll be glad you waited. This cassoulet can be made easily in any home oven, but we recommend cooking it outdoors whenever possible, over a wood fire in your kettle grill or smoker. Even better, we like to bring all of the prepared ingredients when we go camping, and finish it over our campfire.

DAY 1

Cover white beans in cold water and soak overnight.

In a kettle grill, light a two-zone fire (see chapter 1), or prepare smoker and bring temperature to 250°F (121°C).

Arrange shanks, bacon, rib tips, and sausage fatty on a large baking sheet.

To make the dry rub: In a small bowl, mix all rub ingredients and stir to combine. Sprinkle rub over meat.

Smoke for 1 hour, then remove the bacon. Let bacon cool to room temperature and refrigerate. Remove sausage fatty when it reaches an internal temperature of 160°F (71°C), about 2 hours after you began smoking. Let sausage cool to room temperature and refrigerate. Remove shanks and rib tips when meltingly tender (meat will pull away from the bone easily), about 2 hours later. The entire smoking time should be about 4 hours. Let shanks and rib tips cool to room temperature, and refrigerate (A).

FOR CASSOULET:

¼ pound (115 g) salt pork, cubed

2 medium onions, chopped

2 carrots, peeled and cut into ½-inch (1.25-cm) dice

2 ribs celery, cut into ½-inch (1.25-cm) dice

2 tablespoons (30 g) tomato paste

6 cloves garlic, smashed

1 tomato, seeds removed, chopped

2 quarts (1.9 L) reduced-sodium chicken broth

2 bay leaves

1 tablespoon (4.8 g) minced fresh thyme

1 tablespoon (2.5 g) minced fresh sage

FOR GARLIC PANKO TOPPING:

1 cup (115 g) panko crumbs

3 cloves garlic, minced

¼ cup (60 ml) extra-virgin olive oil

¼ cup (15 g) minced parsley

½ cup (1 stick, 112 g) butter, melted (for serving)

DAY 2

Drain the beans. In a kettle grill, light a two-zone fire. When temperature reaches 300°F (150°C) or is very hot (you can't hold your hand over the coals for more than 5 seconds), set a 6-quart (5.7-L) cast-iron pot on the top grill grate near the fire. Let heat for 10 minutes.

To make the cassoulet: Add the salt pork and fry until the pieces are crispy. Remove salt pork and reserve. Add the onions, carrots, and celery to the pot and cook, stirring often, until the onions are translucent, 5 to 8 minutes. Make a "hot spot" in the bottom of the pot by moving the vegetables to the side. Add the tomato paste and garlic to this spot and cook, stirring constantly, for 3 to 5 minutes, or until the tomato paste deepens in color. Stir in the chopped tomatoes, chicken broth, bay leaves, drained beans, pork shanks, bacon, and rib tips. If necessary, add enough cold water to cover beans. Bring to a light boil over the fire.

Take pot off of the grill. Remove top grill grate, and place covered pot on bottom grate. Surround with a mix of lit and unlit charcoal. Cover the grill and cook, maintaining a temperature of 300°F (150°C), for 1½ hours. The beans should be soft but have some texture. If they are still too firm (it's not always easy to maintain an exact temperature in the grill, and the amount of water in the pot varies from pitmaster to pitmaster), you may need to cook for 30 minutes to 1 hour longer. When beans reach the desired consistency, remove the pot from the grill. Remove the bay leaves and fold minced thyme and sage into the beans, stirring gently so as not to break up the beans.

To make the garlic panko topping: In a small bowl, mix panko, garlic, olive oil, and parsley to combine. Set aside until needed.

TO SERVE

Option 1: Remove sausage fatty from the refrigerator and let come to room temperature for 30 minutes.

Slice the fatty and fan on top of the cassoulet. Sprinkle with the panko topping and reserved salt pork, and drizzle melted butter over the top. Return to smoker and cook, uncovered, for 30 minutes or until the topping is nicely browned (B).

Option 2: Cassoulet actually improves with a bit of age. Transfer to a large (12 × 20-inch [30 × 50-cm]) roasting pan. Let cool to room temperature and refrigerate for 1 to 3 days.

When ready to serve, remove cassoulet and sausage from the refrigerator. Preheat oven to 325°F (170°C, or gas mark 3). Slice the sausage fatty and fan on top of the cassoulet. Sprinkle with the reserved salt pork and panko topping, and drizzle melted butter over the top. Bake for 45 minutes, or until warmed through and the top is nicely browned.

YIELD: 12 servings

A: AN EMBARRASSMENT OF PARTY RICHES.

B: CASSOULET SMOKING.

WHAT'S A SAUSAGE FATTY?

WE OFTEN MAKE OUR OWN SAUSAGES, AS DO MOST HARD-CORE BARBECUE FOLKS. A SAUSAGE FATTY IS REALLY NOTHING MORE COMPLICATED THAN A FAT, KIND OF LOOSE, SAUSAGE. WE MAKE THEM WITHOUT CASINGS BECAUSE WE LIKE TO GET A NICE CRUST ON THE MEAT FROM THE DRY RUB. TO SHAPE A FATTY, ROLL THE GROUND MEAT INTO A BIG LOG, WRAP IT TIGHTLY IN PLASTIC, AND REFRIGERATE IT. BEFORE COOKING, REMOVE THE PLASTIC AND COAT THE MEAT IN DRY RUB. WE THINK OURS ARE PRETTY ADDICTIVE. EAT TOO MUCH, THOUGH, AND YOU RUN THE RISK OF BECOMING A SAUSAGE FATTY YOURSELF.

★ GRANDMA WOLFF'S ★ SUPER SMOKED SCRAPPLE

1 quart (946 ml) Smoked Pork Stock (page 117) or low-sodium chicken broth

1½ cups (210 g) quick-cooking (not instant) polenta

Kosher salt and freshly cracked black pepper, to taste

4 cups (946 ml) Basic Pulled Pork (page 118)

1 cup (235 ml) water

1 tablespoon (6 g) dried sage

1 tablespoon (4.3 g) dried thyme

2 tablespoons (28 g) butter (for greasing pans), plus more for frying

1 cup (125 g) flour

Bacon-Cheddar Biscuits (recipe follows)

Fried eggs (as desired)

SPECIAL EQUIPMENT:

Disposable aluminum half-pan, 12¾ × 10⅜ inches (32.4 × 26.4 cm)

Nothing brings back childhood like the aroma of favorite foods. For Chris and his brother, Jamie, it's the smell of slowly frying scrapple and pork roll that their Grandma Wolff used to prepare early in the morning. Of German descent, Grandma Wolff lived near Pennsylvania Dutch country. She served all the regional standards—Lebanon bologna, birch beer, coleslaw, and scrapple. This hearty dish embodies the ethic of not wasting a single "scrap" of food, and often made use of every piece of the hog, from nose to ears to organ meats. Of course, we've added a bit of barbecue love to our version (and left out some less-loved parts). Served with Bacon-Cheddar Biscuits and fried eggs, this is one mind-blowing breakfast.

In a large saucepan over medium heat, bring pork stock to a simmer. Whisk in the polenta and cook for 15 minutes. Season with salt and pepper.

While the polenta is simmering, chop half the pork very fine. Cut the rest into thumb-sized chunks. Mix the meat in a bowl with the water, sage, and thyme. Pour into the polenta mixture and simmer for 30 minutes, stirring constantly.

Grease an aluminum pan. Pour scrapple mixture into the pan, let cool to room temperature, then refrigerate overnight.

Run a knife around the perimeter of the pan and invert onto a cutting board. Cut scrapple in half lengthwise, creating 2 loaves. Slice each loaf into ½-inch (1.3-cm) slices.

Heat a large skillet over medium-high heat and melt a pat of butter. Dredge scrapple slices in flour and fry until crispy on both sides. Serve with Bacon-Cheddar Biscuits and fried eggs.

YIELD: Two 12¾ × 5-inch (32.4 × 13-cm) loaves, serving 18 to 20

Note: Use within 1 week or wrap the loaves and freeze. They will keep frozen for up to 2 months.

BACON-CHEDDAR BISCUITS

½ pound (225 g) sliced bacon

2½ cups (312.5 g) flour, plus extra for cutting

2 teaspoons (9.2 g) baking powder

2 teaspoons (12 g) kosher salt

¼ teaspoon (1.2 g) baking soda

2 tablespoons (28 g) cold vegetable shortening, diced, plus extra for greasing

½ cup (1 stick, 112 g) cold unsalted butter, diced

1½ cup (355 ml) cold buttermilk

½ cup (58 g) sharp Vermont cheddar, shredded finely

These are great with scrapple, on their own with Bacon Jam (page 108) or Honey Butter (page 109), or for breakfast with eggs.

Preheat oven to 425°F (220°C, or gas mark 7).

In a sauté pan over medium-high heat, fry bacon until crisp. Transfer to a paper towel–lined plate to cool, reserving 2 tablespoons (30 ml) bacon fat and chilling until solid. When the bacon is cool enough to handle, crumble with your fingers or mince with a sharp knife and reserve.

In a large mixing bowl, sift together the flour, baking powder, salt, and baking soda. Add the shortening, reserved bacon fat, and butter, and toss to coat. Squeeze bits of shortening, bacon fat, and butter through your fingers until they are the size of large peas (or use 2 knives or a pastry blender to cut into the flour).

Make a well in the center of the flour and pour in the buttermilk. Stir with light, quick strokes until the dough is just combined, but do not overwork. The dough will be very sticky.

Sprinkle your hands and a work surface liberally with flour and transfer the dough to the floured surface. Quickly pat the dough to an even 1-inch (2.5-cm) thickness. Dip a sharp, 2-inch (5-cm) biscuit or cookie cutter into the flour, then cut out the biscuits, reflouring as needed. If necessary, very gently gather any large scraps together, without squeezing the dough, and cut more biscuits. Transfer to a well-greased 9 × 13-inch (23 × 33-cm) baking sheet. Equally and evenly sprinkle the cheddar, then the crumbled bacon, over each biscuit.

Bake biscuits until light golden brown, 15 to 20 minutes. Serve hot.

YIELD: 12 large biscuits

★ POPCORN ICE CREAM SANDWICHES ★

24 D.I.Y. Vanilla Wafers (recipe follows)

1 cup (235 ml) Popcorn Ice Cream,
or more to taste (recipe follows)

Whiskey Caramel Sauce, for dipping
(recipe follows)

Andy started serving Popcorn Ice Cream in his restaurant as an experimental dessert and, to the surprise of a few naysayers (including one on this team who shall remain nameless), it was a blowout hit. We also had this great recipe for D.I.Y. Vanilla Wafers, and the temptation to scoop a little ice cream onto a cookie, then slap another cookie on top was too tough to resist. Dunking the finished product in our Whiskey Caramel Sauce was a no-brainer. The beauty of this dessert is that you can mix and match the individual parts, so if you want to make the ice cream but don't feel like sandwiches, that's okay. Or even if you make the ice cream and cookies but don't freeze them together, you can still serve them as one dessert. The ice cream should steep overnight, for the full popcorn flavor to penetrate. And the vanilla flavor in the cookies intensifies after a day or two, so you can make them ahead to break up your workload.

Line a baking sheet with foil or parchment paper.

Place 12 vanilla wafers, flat-side up, on the baking sheet, and top each one with a small scoop of slightly softened ice cream. Immediately place another cookie right side up on top of the ice cream, and press gently. Repeat with remaining cookies and ice cream and freeze on the baking sheet until firm, or overnight. Transfer the frozen sandwiches to a resealable plastic container and keep frozen until ready to serve.

Serve ice cream sandwiches with Whiskey Caramel Sauce for dipping. You can also serve the ice cream, cookies, and sauce separately, and allow guests to make their own cookie sundaes, or popcorn-caramel ice cream sundaes with vanilla wafers on the side. With desserts like this, you really don't want to be too controlling.

YIELD: 12 ice cream sandwiches

D.I.Y. VANILLA WAFERS

4 tablespoons (55 g) butter, softened

3 tablespoons (42 g) vegetable shortening

½ cup (100 g) granulated sugar

½ cup (60 g) powdered sugar

1 vanilla bean, seeds only

1 teaspoon (5 ml) vanilla extract

¼ teaspoon (1.5 g) salt

2 egg whites

1½ cups (187.5 g) cake flour

1 teaspoon (4.6 g) baking powder

1 tablespoon (15 ml) milk

These cookies will bring out your inner child, but they're far superior to the boxed version you grew up with.

Preheat oven to 325°F (170°C, or gas mark 3). Line a baking sheet with parchment paper, and grease the parchment or coat with nonstick spray.

In the bowl of a stand mixer fitted with the paddle attachment, cream together the butter and shortening. Add the sugars, vanilla bean seeds, extract, and salt, and continue beating until the mixture is very light and creamy.

In a separate bowl, whip egg whites to form stiff peaks. Add them to the butter mixture, and beat just to incorporate.

With the mixer on low speed, add the flour and baking powder, scraping down the sides of the bowl as needed. Add the milk and continue mixing until dough looks smooth and silky.

Drop the dough by 1- to 1½-inch (2.5- to 3.6-cm) rounded spoonfuls onto the prepared baking sheet, about 2 inches (5 cm) apart.

Bake until cookies are lightly colored on top and the edges are golden brown, 15 to 18 minutes. Remove to a wire rack to cool.

YIELD: 24 cookies

POPCORN ICE CREAM

2 tablespoons (18 g) popcorn kernels

1 tablespoon (15 ml) vegetable oil

1½ cups (355 ml) half-and-half

1½ cups (355 ml) heavy cream

1 vanilla bean, split

6 large egg yolks

1 cup (200 g) sugar

2 teaspoons (6 g) sea salt

SPECIAL EQUIPMENT:

Ice cream maker

Place popcorn and oil in a 2-quart (1.9-L) saucepan and shake frequently over medium-high heat by moving back and forth on the burner. When the first kernel pops, after 1 to 3 minutes, cover pan and continue shaking, until the popping slows to 1 to 2 pops every 10 seconds. Be careful not to burn the popcorn. Remove from heat and transfer to a bowl.

In a heavy-bottomed saucepan over medium heat, warm the half-and-half, heavy cream, and vanilla bean just until you see small bubbles form around the edges of the pan. Remove from heat and set aside.

In the bowl of an electric mixer fitted with the paddle attachment, beat the egg yolks and sugar on medium speed until thick and light, 2 to 3 minutes. (You can also use an electric hand mixer or whisk, but double the time.)

With the mixer on medium speed, gradually add about half of the hot cream, beating until smooth. Pour the contents of the mixer bowl into the remaining cream in the saucepan, and mix well.

Place the pan over medium-low heat and cook, stirring constantly, until the mixture registers just barely 180°F (82°C) on an instant-read thermometer and is thick enough to coat the back of a spoon, about 15 minutes. Watch carefully, stirring constantly and scraping the bottom of the pan. Don't let the mixture boil or go over 180°F (82°C), or it will curdle.

Remove pan from heat and fish out the vanilla bean. Pour custard into metal bowl and stir in popcorn. Cover and refrigerate for 12 to 24 hours.

Strain popcorn custard through a fine-mesh strainer into a bowl, pressing down on the popcorn. Churn in an ice cream maker, following the manufacturer's instructions. When ice cream is almost frozen, add sea salt.

YIELD: 1 quart (946 ml)

WHISKEY CARAMEL SAUCE

¾ cup (1½ sticks, 167 g) unsalted butter, divided

2 cups (400 g) sugar

¼ cup (60 ml) water

3 tablespoons (45 ml) light corn syrup

2 teaspoons (12 g) salt

1 cup (235 ml) heavy cream

½ cup (120 ml) your favorite whiskey, divided

SPECIAL EQUIPMENT:

Candy thermometer

This recipe makes more sauce than you will need, but it's a great, versatile topping that will keep in the refrigerator for at least a couple of weeks and is delicious on ice cream, puddings, or even by the spoonful.

In a 2- or 3-quart (1.9- or 2.8-L) heavy-bottomed saucepan, melt ½ cup (1 stick, 112 g) of the butter over medium heat. Add the sugar, water, corn syrup, and salt, and continue to cook over medium heat, stirring to help dissolve the sugar. Attach a candy thermometer to the pan, increase the heat to medium-high, and continue to cook, stirring frequently with a heat-proof spatula, until the temperature reaches 295 to 300°F (146 to 150°C).

Carefully add the cream all at once (mixture will steam and bubble up), stirring to dissolve the caramel, and remove from heat. Add ¼ cup (60 ml) of the whiskey and the remaining ¼ cup (55 g) butter and mix well. Allow to cool slightly, and taste the caramel, adding more whiskey if desired, 1 tablespoon (15 ml) at a time, to taste (you may not need all of the whiskey).

YIELD: 3 cups (710 ml)

★ CHAPTER 7 ★

ROAD TRIP

COMPETITION BARBECUE takes us all over the United States, but we also love to travel for the sheer pleasure of it within and beyond the confines of our diverse nation. Naturally, wherever we are, we are pretty focused on finding the best available local cuisine— by which we mean what the neighborhood folks are eating every day, as well as what's being served in the four-star restaurants. Depending on the country we're in, the best local food is usually sold on the street, from food trucks, at roadside stands, or in family-run eateries. When we get home, we like to recreate, as best we can, the food we loved while we were away—both as a way to extend our own pleasure and to share it with people who didn't get to come with us.

Recipes in this chapter were inspired by food that blew us away from all over the world. Some were made from what were, to us, unusual ingredients we didn't necessarily think we were going to like: whole pig's head, anyone? Most of them are made from inexpensive ingredients and cuts of meat—like barbecue. They are often made by people who stand outside all night, cooking in the elements—like barbecue. They are loaded with flavor and rich in local tradition—like barbecue. This is probably why the food rings so true to us and why we're so drawn to it.

We've adapted some of our favorite discoveries to dishes you can make in your home smokers and grills and serve to family and friends. That pig's head? It's a show-stopper at a party, with our Jungle Curry and lettuce wrappers. Korean-Style BBQ Beef Sandwiches, already a hit at food trucks in Los Angeles, are easy to make at home. And we have an absolutely wicked version of tacos al pastor, classic Mexican street food, that your friends are not likely to forget.

So hit the road—even if it's just in your backyard.

★ AL PASTOR TACOS DIABOLO ★

FOR BRINE:

2 quarts (1.9 L) pineapple juice

4 dried amarillo or ancho chile peppers, stems removed and chopped (wear gloves)

8 dried ghost chiles, stems removed and chopped (wear gloves)

2 tablespoons (32 g) tomato paste

½ cup (120 ml) white vinegar

1 bunch cilantro, chopped

1 tablespoon (2.1 g) cumin seeds, toasted and ground

½ cup (120 g) molasses

4 cloves garlic, minced

2 tablespoons (36 g) kosher salt

FOR AL PASTOR:

2 pounds (1 kg) boneless pork shoulder or butt

Kosher salt and freshly cracked black pepper, to taste

FOR TACOS:

12 corn tortillas

½ head iceberg lettuce (or napa cabbage), shredded

1 cup (120 g) queso fresco, crumbled

Salsa Roja (recipe follows)

6 limes

2 bunches fresh cilantro, roughly chopped

Andy's restaurant, Tremont 647, is known for its $2 Taco Tuesdays. A menu regular is Tacos from Hell, featuring ghost chiles, rated among the hottest in the world on the Scoville scale. Our Al Pastor Tacos Diabolo, a twist on the 647 version, also feature ghost chiles—they're as tasty as they are killer. If you want to tone them down a bit, substitute pasilla or New Mexican green chiles. Whichever you use, it's important to take as much care handling them as eating them.

To make the brine: In a large stockpot over high heat, bring the brine ingredients to a boil and continue to cook for 5 minutes. Transfer to a bowl and refrigerate, covered, until cool but not too cold (a thermometer inserted into the liquid should not register lower than 42°F [5°C]).

To make the al pastor: Place pork in a large bowl and pour brine over it. Cover and refrigerate for 1 to 3 days.

Remove pork from brine. Season liberally with salt and pepper.

In kettle grill or smoker, build a two-zone fire (see chapter 1). When you can only hold your hand above the fire for 5 seconds, place the pork close to but not over it, and cover. Grill roast the pork for 10 minutes, then turn over and rotate. Continue to roast, turning and rotating every 10 minutes, for 30 to 40 minutes, or until pork reaches 170°F (77°C) internally. Transfer to a large cutting board and let it rest.

To make the tacos: Heat the tortillas over the grill for about 30 seconds per side. Transfer to a plate and cover with foil. Chop pork into bite-size pieces or slice it.

Arrange tortillas on a serving platter. Place some shredded lettuce or cabbage, pork, and queso fresco on each one. Drizzle with Salsa Roja and a squeeze of lime, and sprinkle with cilantro. Fold in half. Eat warm.

YIELD: 4 to 6 appetizer servings

SALSA ROJA

2 tablespoons (30 ml) extra-virgin olive oil

2 cloves garlic, chopped

2 plum tomatoes, cored and cut in half

1 medium yellow onion, sliced ½ inch (1.3 cm) thick

2 tomatillos, cored

2 ghost chiles, stems removed (wear gloves)

¼ cup (60 ml) fresh lime juice (from 1½ to 2 limes)

Kosher salt and freshly cracked black pepper, to taste

Preheat oven to 400°F (200°C, or gas mark 6).

Coat the bottom of an 8 × 8-inch (20 × 20-cm) baking pan with oil. Combine the garlic, tomatoes, onion, and tomatillos in the pan and bake for 20 minutes. Add ghost chiles and bake for 5 minutes more.

Remove from oven and transfer vegetables to a blender. Add lime juice, and purée until smooth. Season with salt and pepper.

Serve warm or cold. Salsa will last up to 4 days in the refrigerator in a tightly sealed container.

YIELD: Approximately 2 cups (470 ml)

BEWARE OF GHOST (CHILE)S

GHOST CHILES, OR BHUT JOLOKIA, ARE NATIVE TO NORTHEAST INDIA. SOME PEOPLE SAY THE ENGLISH NAME IS A DIRECT TRANSLATION OF THE INDIAN. OTHERS SAY IT CAME ABOUT BECAUSE THE PEPPERS ARE SO HOT THAT WHEN YOU EAT ONE YOU'LL WISH YOU WERE DEAD. EITHER WAY, AS WITH MANY HOT PEPPERS, IT'S REALLY IMPORTANT TO BE CAREFUL HANDLING THEM. WHEN CHOPPING OR CUTTING, IN PARTICULAR, YOU SHOULD WEAR GLOVES BECAUSE THE OLEORESIN FROM THE CHILES WILL STICK TO YOUR HANDS. IF YOU TOUCH YOUR EYES, NOSE, OR—WE SHUDDER TO THINK—OTHER SENSITIVE AREAS, YOU REALLY MAY FEEL AS IF YOU'VE SEEN A GHOST. OR BECOME ONE.

WE RECOMMEND SIMILAR CAUTION WHEN EATING THESE BABIES. PARTICULARLY IF YOU HAVEN'T TRIED THEM BEFORE, START SMALL. IN INDIA, GHOST CHILES ARE USED TO TREAT STOMACH AILMENTS, AS A WAY TO BEAT THE INTENSE SUMMER HEAT (BECAUSE THEY PROVOKE SUCH INTENSE PERSPIRATION), AND AS A LAXATIVE. NEED WE SAY MORE?

★ "LORD OF THE FLIES" ROAST ★
WITH JUNGLE CURRY LETTUCE WRAPS

FOR PIG'S HEAD:

1 whole pig's head, available by special order from your butcher or local farmer

Kosher salt and freshly cracked black pepper, to taste

FOR RUB:

½ cup (115 g) firmly packed light brown sugar

2 star anise, ground

2 tablespoons (10 g) coriander seeds, toasted and ground

1½ teaspoons (3.5 g) cinnamon

2 tablespoons (36 g) kosher salt

1½ teaspoons (6 g) garlic powder

FOR BASTING LIQUID:

1 cup (235 ml) honey

1 cup (235 ml) water

2 Kaffir lime leaves, chopped

2 stalks lemongrass, cut on the diagonal into 3-inch (7.5-cm) pieces

2 tablespoons (11 g) ground ginger

¼ cup (60 ml) fish sauce

Trust us, people will always remember you for serving a whole pig's head—or several—on a platter. It's a great party appetizer, not to mention conversation starter. And it could trigger some unexpected associations. But once your guests dig in—and we do mean that literally— any thoughts of pigs' heads on sticks and high school English class will give way to the simple sensations of sweet cheek and neck meat, offset by spicy curry, wrapped in lettuce leaves, in their mouths. A word of caution: You might want to leave your vegetarian friends off this particular guest list.

To make the pig's head: Prepare smoker and bring heat to 350°F (180°C). This can also be done in a gas grill by turning on one side and bringing the temperature to 350°F (180°C), and keeping the other side turned off.

Remove hair from pig's head by carefully shaving it, or singeing over fire. (We prefer to shave him. It's so much more dignified.) Sprinkle head liberally with salt and pepper, and smoke, covered, for 1½ hours (A). If using a gas grill, place head on the cooler side.

While the head is smoking, make the rub and basting liquid.

To make the rub: In a small bowl, mix all rub ingredients until well blended, and set aside.

To make the basting liquid: In a medium bowl, stir all ingredients until combined. Set aside.

A: SPRINKLE HEAD WITH SALT AND PEPPER
AND SMOKE, COVERED.

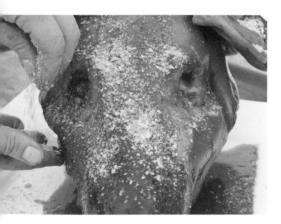

B: REMOVE FROM SMOKER AND POUR
BASTING LIQUID OVER HEAD.

C: READY FOR MY CLOSE-UP.

"LORD OF THE FLIES" ROAST WITH JUNGLE CURRY LETTUCE WRAPS (CONTINUED)

FOR WRAPS:

4 heads Bibb lettuce, leaves only,
stacked on a plate

Jungle Curry (recipe follows)

½ cup (8 g) cilantro leaves

1 bunch scallions, cut into
¼-inch (6-mm) rings

8 limes, cut into wedges

Hot sauce, such as Sriracha (optional)

SPECIAL EQUIPMENT:

Disposable razor

After 1½ hours, remove the head from the smoker and place on a cutting board or sheet pan lined with a large piece of aluminum foil (about 3 feet [90 cm] long). Pour about three-quarters of the basting liquid over the head (B). Wrap head in foil, making sure it is completely covered, and return to smoker for 1½ hours, or until the cheeks have an internal temperature of at least 190°F (88°C). Remove from smoker, unwrap the foil, pour remaining basting liquid over head, and sprinkle with rub (C). Allow to cool slightly.

To make the wraps: Transfer the pig's head to a very large serving platter with the lettuce leaves, curry, cilantro, scallions, lime wedges, and hot sauce set in bowls around it. Let your friends pull off the meat and customize their own wraps.

YIELD: 8 to 10 appetizer servings

Note: If you are squeamish about cooking a pig's head, substitute pork butts. It would be a shame to miss out on these wicked flavors.

JUNGLE CURRY

1 tablespoon (15 ml) vegetable oil

1 tablespoon (6 g) minced fresh ginger

3 cloves garlic, minced

One 14-ounce (425-ml) can
unsweetened coconut milk

2 cups (475 ml) low-sodium chicken broth
or Smoked Pork Stock (page 117)

3-inch (7.5-cm) piece lemongrass,
split in half lengthwise

2 tablespoons (12.6 g) curry powder

3 Kaffir lime leaves

8 Thai chiles, stems removed (wear gloves)

2 star anise

1 tablespoon (5 g) coriander seeds, toasted

1 bunch cilantro

3 tablespoons (45 ml) fresh lime juice

Fish sauce, to taste

In a saucepan over medium heat, combine oil, ginger, and garlic and stir for 2 to 4 minutes, until fragrant but not brown. Add the coconut milk, broth, lemongrass, curry, lime leaves, chiles, star anise, and coriander seeds, turn heat to medium-high, and simmer for 20 minutes, stirring occasionally. Remove from heat. Stir in cilantro and steep for 5 minutes. Strain. Season with lime juice and fish sauce.

YIELD: About 3 cups (710 ml)

★ KOREAN-STYLE ★
BBQ BEEF SANDWICH

3 pounds (1.37 kg) skirt, flank, or chuck steak

Korean Beef Marinade (recipe follows)

1 cup (235 ml) Korean BBQ Sauce (recipe follows)

1 bunch scallions, chopped
(white and green parts)

2 tablespoons (16.2 g) sesame seeds

1 lime

10 torta or bolillo rolls (available in Mexican
markets, but any crusty sandwich rolls will work)

1½ cups (340 g) mayonnaise (we prefer Kewpie
mayonnaise, found in many Asian markets)

2 cups (230 g) shredded Monterey Jack cheese

1½ cups (355 ml) Three-Day BBQ Kimchi
(page 169) or prepared kimchi
(found in many Asian markets)

1 head romaine lettuce, shredded

1 cup (235 ml) bottled Caesar salad dressing

SPECIAL EQUIPMENT:

Disposable aluminum pan

On one late-night R & D foray to our favorite Los Angeles food truck, we were inspired by a great combination of the Korean staples beef bulgogi and kimchi, which were served with Mexican torta rolls, Caesar salad, and lots of melted cheese. Here is our take on this tasty concoction.

Place the steaks in a large resealable plastic bag. Pour in marinade and close the bag, being careful to keep out as much air as possible. Place the bag in a deep bowl and refrigerate for 24 hours, turning occasionally.

In a kettle grill, build a two-zone charcoal fire. Remove steaks from the marinade and transfer to a strainer to remove excess liquid. Discard marinade.

When you are just able to hold your hand over the coals for 5 seconds, grill steaks for about 3 minutes per side, until nicely caramelized. Watch carefully, because the sugar in the marinade can burn. Move steaks to the cool side of the grill and cook until they register an internal temperature of 140°F (60°C). Remove from grill and let rest for 15 minutes.

Slice meat thinly, against the grain. Transfer to a disposable aluminum pan, pour the Korean BBQ Sauce over the meat, sprinkle with scallions and sesame seeds, and squeeze fresh lime juice over all. Cover the pan.

Brush the rolls lightly with mayonnaise and grill for 2 to 3 minutes, until crispy.

Spread more mayonnaise on one side of the rolls, then mound sliced beef on top. Spoon some of the Korean BBQ Sauce from the pan over the beef, add cheese, kimchi, shredded romaine, and a drizzle of Caesar dressing, then top with the other half of the roll. Wrap each sandwich tightly in foil and set down on the cooler side of the grill just until the cheese melts, about 5 minutes. Unwrap and dig in.

YIELD: 10 sandwiches

KOREAN BEEF MARINADE

1 cup (235 ml) light soy sauce

½ cup (75 g) packed light brown sugar

¼ cup (60 ml) honey

2 tablespoons (30 ml) dark sesame oil

10 cloves garlic, smashed

3-inch (7.5-cm) piece ginger, unpeeled and sliced

6 scallions, chopped

1 tablespoon (15 ml) hot chili sauce, such as Sriracha

1 tablespoon (8 g) sesame seeds

Mix all ingredients in a bowl and stir to combine.

YIELD: About 2 cups (470 ml)

KOREAN BBQ SAUCE

¼ cup (60 ml) amber agave nectar or honey

¼ cup (60 ml) soy sauce

¼ cup (60 ml) pear juice

2 tablespoons (40 g) Korean chili sauce

2 teaspoons (10 ml) rice wine vinegar

2 teaspoons (10 ml) sesame oil

1 clove garlic, minced

1 teaspoon (2 g) minced fresh ginger

1 teaspoon (5 ml) hot chili sauce, such as Sriracha

In a small saucepan over high heat, bring all ingredients to a boil. Reduce heat to low and simmer for 15 minutes. Remove from heat and let cool to room temperature. Store in a squeeze bottle.

YIELD: About 1 cup (235 ml)

★ YAKITORI-GLAZED FISH COLLAR ★

FOR FISH:

7 cups (1.7 L) water

1 cup (150 g) palm sugar (or brown sugar)

1 cup (235 ml) soy sauce

1 cup (40 g) loosely packed Thai basil leaves

½ cup (50 g) roughly chopped fresh ginger

5 star anise

¼ cup (25 g) white peppercorns, cracked

1 whole cinnamon stick

Zest of 4 limes

Zest of 4 clementines (or oranges)

1 yellowtail* (or salmon) collar, 1 to 2 pounds (455 to 910 g)

FOR YAKITORI GLAZE:

½ cup (120 ml) sake

¾ cup (175 ml) soy sauce

¼ cup (60 ml) yuzu juice (or a mix of half lime, half orange juice)

½ cup (120 ml) mirin

½ cup (115 g) packed light brown sugar

1 teaspoon (2.7 g) grated fresh ginger

1 teaspoon (1.8 g) coriander seeds, toasted and ground

Sesame Crackers (recipe follows)

Cilantro leaves, minced chives, lime wedges, and chile garlic paste (such as sambal oelek), for garnish

This dish is designed for parties and festive gatherings. Though you rarely see fish collar listed, it is one of our favorite parts of the fish because the meat is so flaky and creamy. Most fishmongers will either have it or can get it for you. The Yakitori Glaze is a great finishing sauce for all grilled foods, from fish to chicken to vegetables. We suggest making the Sesame Crackers while the collar is brining, so everything is ready at the same time.

To make the fish: In a large stockpot over high heat, bring water and next 9 ingredients (through clementine zest) to a boil and continue to cook for 5 minutes. Remove from heat. Transfer brine to a large bowl and cool completely.

Place fish collar in bowl, pour brine over it, and let brine for 2 hours.

To make the glaze: In a medium saucepan over medium-high heat, bring all glaze ingredients to a boil. Lower heat and cook until liquid is reduced by half, about 40 minutes. Transfer to a bowl, cover, and refrigerate until ready to use.

Prepare smoker and bring temperature to 325°F (170°C). Remove yellowtail collar from brine and smoke for 40 to 50 minutes, or until internal temperature reaches 140°F (60°C) (salmon may take up to twice as long). Halfway through smoking, liberally brush the collar with glaze. Brush with glaze again after fish has finished cooking.

Place the collar on a large plate and drizzle any remaining Yakitori Glaze over it. Use a fork and butter knife to remove the meat from the bone, place on Sesame Crackers, and allow guests to sprinkle with the garnishes they choose.

YIELD: 4 to 6 appetizer servings, but recipe can be doubled

* Yellowtail is found at many Asian markets.

SESAME CRACKERS

1½ cups (355 ml) water

½ cup (95 g) brown rice

1 teaspoon (6 g) salt

2 tablespoons (16 g) black sesame seeds

½ teaspoon (1 g) ground cumin

In a 2-quart (1.9-L) saucepan over high heat, combine water, rice, and salt and bring to a boil. Turn down the heat until just barely simmering. Cover and cook for 45 minutes to 1 hour, until rice is tender. Stir in sesame seeds and cumin. Remove from heat and allow to cool for about 15 minutes.

Preheat oven to 325°F (170°C, or gas mark 3). Grease a baking sheet and line with parchment paper.

With wet hands, form rice dough into 18 small balls, and flatten into 2-inch (5-cm) rounds, about ¼ inch (6 mm) thick, on the prepared baking sheet.

Bake for 45 minutes, until crackers are browned and crispy on the outside. Remove from oven and let cool on the sheet pan for 1 minute before removing to a wire rack to cool completely. Use within a few hours; crackers soften if stored.

YIELD: 18 crackers

FISH COLLAR

FISH COLLAR IS THE FATTY MEAT JUST BEHIND THE GILLS. IT IS VERY SWEET AND SUPPLE. BECAUSE IT DOES NOT LOOK PARTICULARLY APPETIZING, AND A LOT OF PEOPLE IN THE UNITED STATES ARE NOT FAMILIAR WITH THE CUT, IT IS A VASTLY UNDERUTILIZED PIECE OF FISH. IN JAPAN, IT IS CONSIDERED THE *FOIE GRAS* OF THE SEA. IT IS BEST GRILLED OR ROASTED.

★ PORK JOWL TORTILLA ★

2 pork jowls, about ¼ pound (115 g) each

¼ cup (25 g) IQUE Dry Rub (page 32)

1 large onion, sliced ¼ inch (6 mm) thick

1 cup (235 ml) olive oil, divided

3 cloves garlic, minced

4 medium Yukon gold potatoes, peeled and sliced ¼ inch (6 mm) thick

8 eggs

2 teaspoons (12 g) salt

½ teaspoon (1 g) ground pepper

Parsley Aioli (recipe follows)

The simple tortilla Española, or Spanish potato omelet, is a staple that made its way to the United States with the tapas incursion. As with any imported tradition, changes have been made along the way. But we don't think any Spaniard would object too strenuously to our addition of smoked pork jowl, which adds delightful richness to this dish. Serve it for brunch, hot or at room temperature. You can get jowls, or cheeks, from your specialty butcher.

Prepare smoker and bring temperature to 250°F (120°C).

Dust the pork jowls with rub and smoke for 2 to 3 hours, or until an internal temperature registers 175°F (79°C). Remove from smoker and let cool. When cool enough to handle, slice thinly (about ⅛ inch, or 3 mm, thick).

Preheat oven to 325°F (170°C, or gas mark 3).

In a 12-inch (30-cm) nonstick, ovenproof skillet over medium heat, sauté onion in ¾ cup (175 ml) of the olive oil until translucent, 3 to 4 minutes, then add garlic and cook for 2 minutes more. With a slotted spoon, transfer onion and garlic to a large bowl, leaving the oil in the pan.

Raise heat to medium-high and add enough potato slices to cover the bottom of the skillet. Sear for 2 minutes, then turn over and cook for 2 minutes more. Remove potatoes with a slotted spoon and add to onion mixture. Repeat until all potatoes are cooked.

In a separate bowl, beat the eggs with the salt and pepper. Add potatoes, onions, and sliced pork. Stir to thoroughly coat all ingredients with the eggs.

Clean skillet and heat the remaining ¼ cup (60 ml) olive oil over medium-high heat. Using a slotted spoon, scoop half the potatoes out of the egg mixture and transfer to the skillet, spreading them out to cover the bottom in an even layer. Pour half the egg mixture over the potatoes. Repeat with the remaining potatoes and the remaining egg mixture. Place the skillet in the preheated oven and cook for 20 to 25 minutes, until a knife slides in easily.

Remove tortilla from oven and let cool for 5 minutes. Place a baking sheet over the top of the skillet and quickly flip over to remove tortilla. (You might want to bang on the bottom of the pan, when inverted, with a wooden spoon to make sure it does not stick.) Let cool for 5 minutes more.

Cut the tortilla into 6 or 8 wedges and serve hot or cold with a small dollop of Parsley Aioli. For a larger gathering, you could cut it into smaller pieces and arrange on a tray or serve as passed appetizers.

YIELD: 6 to 8 appetizer or light main course servings, or 12 one-bite appetizers

PARSLEY AIOLI

2 cups (120 g) parsley leaves

1 cup (235 ml) olive oil

2 cloves garlic, minced

2 egg yolks

1 teaspoon (5 ml) Dijon mustard

3 tablespoons (45 ml) fresh lemon juice

Kosher salt and freshly cracked black pepper, to taste

In a large saucepan over high heat, bring salted water to a boil. Have a bowl of ice water ready. Place the parsley leaves in a sieve and dip into boiling water for 30 seconds. Quickly dip the sieve in the ice water and hold for another 30 seconds, until the parsley is cold. Remove sieve from the ice water and press gently on the parsley to remove water. Place parsley between two paper towels and pat dry. Transfer parsley to a blender, add oil and garlic, and purée until smooth.

In the bowl of a stand mixer with a whisk attachment, beat egg yolks on medium-high until light and doubled in volume, 3 to 4 minutes. Add the mustard and lemon juice, and beat for 1 minute more. Decrease mixer speed to medium, and slowly stream in the parsley oil until mixture is thick. Season with salt and pepper. Transfer to a bowl, cover, and refrigerate until needed.

YIELD: 1¼ cups (355 ml)

★ SMOKED OXTAIL AND CHEESY ★ POTATO GRATIN

FOR OXTAIL:

5 to 7 pounds (2.27 to 3.18 kg) oxtail

Kosher salt and freshly cracked black pepper, to taste

FOR GRATIN:

1 cup (235 ml) heavy cream

¼ cup (4 g) minced chives

3 large chipotle peppers in adobo, minced (about 2 tablespoons [30 ml])

6 medium Yukon gold potatoes (about 2 pounds [1 kg]), peeled and sliced ⅛ inch (3 mm) thick

Kosher salt and freshly cracked black pepper

¾ cup (88 g) grated extra-sharp Vermont cheddar

¾ cup (90 g) grated Gruyère cheese

1 cup (115 g) panko bread crumbs

¼ cup (25 g) grated Parmigiano-Reggiano

2 tablespoons (28 g) butter, melted

¼ cup (15 g) chopped parsley

Chefs love oxtail because it's rich and hearty. But it's a delicacy that is worth learning about for home cooks, too. This is not a quick-prep dish. Like any part of an animal that gets a lot of exercise, oxtail needs a long time to cook. It's worth waiting for because once it starts to break down, it has a beautiful, luscious flavor. Combining it with the potato gratin turns a simple grilled steak into an over-the-top indulgence. Paired with a green salad or vegetable, this is a perfect meal.

To make the oxtail: Prepare smoker and bring to 225°F (107°C).

Season the oxtail well with salt and pepper. Smoke for 4 hours. Remove from smoker. When cool enough to handle, pull or cut the meat off the bones and remove any cartilage. Chop the meat and wrap tightly in aluminum foil. Smoke for 30 minutes more. Remove from smoker, unwrap, and strain excess fat in a colander while you prepare the gratin.

To make the gratin: Preheat oven or smoker to 400°F (200°C, or gas mark 6). Grease a 9 × 13-inch (23 × 33-cm) baking dish.

In a large bowl, combine the cream, chives, chipotle, and potato slices, and liberally season with salt and pepper.

In a separate bowl, mix the cheddar and Gruyère.

Layer the potatoes in the prepared baking dish, alternating with cheese mixture and chopped oxtail. Pour the remaining cream mixture over the top.

In a small bowl, combine the bread crumbs, Parmigiano, butter, and parsley and sprinkle over potato mixture. Bake in the center of the oven or smoker until the potatoes are easily pierced by a knife and the crumbs are golden brown on top, 45 minutes to 1 hour.

YIELD: 10 to 12 servings

★ MACGYVER JULEP ★

FOR 1 DRINK:

1 sprig fresh mint

1 ounce (28 ml) coffee pot simple syrup*

2 ounces (60 ml) bourbon

Crushed ice

FOR 22 THIRSTY PEOPLE:

1 bunch of mint

22 ounces (630 ml) coffee pot simple syrup*

Two 750-ml bottles of bourbon

Crushed ice

We'll go anywhere we have to for a barbecue competition—and the occasional championship game—so we frequently find ourselves stranded in out-of-the-way strip mall motels with little in the way of local resources. But a person's gotta drink, and our standards in that department are just as high as they are for what we eat. Fortunately, one of our closest friends, Jackson Cannon, happens to be the bar director at Eastern Standard in Boston—and an acclaimed mixologist. Not only has he provided us with clever solutions for making do with whatever we find in our motel rooms (see sidebar), but he also created the inspired cocktail recipes for this book.

For 1 drink: Separate mint crowns and reserve for garnish.

Place mint in the bottom of the serving glass. Add simple syrup and gently press mint into the syrup with a spoon. Add bourbon and steep for 5 minutes or up to several hours. When ready to serve, add crushed ice and garnish with mint crown.

For 22 thirsty people: Separate mint crowns and reserve for garnish.

To serve punch style, make the "muddle" (stir together the syrup, bourbon, and mint and crush the mint leaves with a spoon) in one large bowl ahead of time. As the party starts, crush ice and provide next to the muddle with available glassware or plastic cups, and mint garnish on the side. Allow guests to serve themselves.

YIELD: 1 drink or 22

* If you don't happen to be in a hotel, you can prepare simple syrup the traditional way. Bring equal amounts of water and sugar to a boil in a saucepan, stirring until sugar is completely dissolved. Let cool completely.

MAKING SIMPLE SYRUP AND OTHER COCKTAIL NECESSITIES IN YOUR MOTEL ROOM

SAY YOU'RE FROM NEW ENGLAND AND YOU'RE IN A BARBECUE COMPETITION IN TENNESSEE, OR YOUR FOOTBALL TEAM (WE'LL JUST SAY NEW ENGLAND AGAIN) IS IN THE SUPER BOWL AND YOU SNAGGED TICKETS TO SEE THEM. YOU HAVE A FABULOUS TAILGATE PLANNED AND YOU WANT YOUR COCKTAILS TO LIVE UP TO THE FOOD. BECAUSE TRANSPORTING LIQUIDS BY AIR IS A BIT TOUGH THESE DAYS, YOU'RE GOING TO HAVE TO MAKE EVERYTHING ON SITE. NO KITCHEN? NO PROBLEM. YOU CAN MAKE INGREDIENTS FOR ARTISANAL COCKTAILS EVEN IN YOUR MOTEL ROOM.

FOR SIMPLE SYRUP, PREPARE THE COFFEE POT BY RUNNING IT ONCE WITH ONLY HOT WATER TO CLEAN IT. THEN PLACE 2 CUPS (470 ML) OF WATER IN THE BACK OF THE POT READY FOR "BREWING," AND 2 CUPS (400 G) OF SUGAR IN THE ACTUAL COFFEE POT (NEVER IN THE BACK). YOU'LL HAVE TO EYEBALL THIS, BECAUSE IT'S DOUBTFUL YOU'LL BE TRAVELING WITH MEASURING CUPS AND EVEN MORE UNLIKELY YOUR ROOM WILL HAVE THEM. "BREW" THE HOT WATER INTO THE SUGAR AND STIR WHEN IT'S DONE. SET ASIDE TO COOL. FOR HERBAL SYRUPS, LIKE TARRAGON, THYME, AND MINT, PLACE THE HERBS IN THE POT WITH THE SUGAR AND LET THEM STEEP IN THERE WHILE COOLING.

ANOTHER COCKTAIL NECESSITY: CRUSHING ICE WITHOUT THE ASSISTANCE OF FANCY EQUIPMENT IS A SNAP! FIRST, TAPE A HAMMER OR AN AUTO WRENCH TO A TOWEL, FOR PAD-DING. FOR SINGLE SERVINGS, WRAP A FISTFUL OR TWO OF ICE IN A SMALL TOWEL AND SMASH WITH THE PREPARED HAMMER OR WRENCH. FOR LARGER AMOUNTS, FILL A PILLOW-CASE WITH ICE AND SMASH WITH THE SAME HAMMER OR WRENCH.

★ MOTEL 6 OLD-FASHIONED ★

2 packets sugar (usually found next to motel room's coffeemaker)

2 dashes bitters (your favorite)

2 ounces (60 ml) whiskey (any kind)

Ice

Citrus peel (lemon, orange, and grapefruit work best)

You don't have to be in a motel room to make this drink. But if you are, and there isn't a good bar for miles around, you don't have to suffer. Good bitters add a lot to the mix. Angostura and Peychaud's are always good choices.

Put the sugar from the packets in a to-go coffee cup. Add dashes of bitters and a splash of tap water. Stir vigorously to create a kind of paste at the bottom. Add whiskey and stir vigorously again. Add a scoop of ice and stir gently.

Garnish with piece of citrus peel. Cheers!

YIELD: 1 drink

★ TEA TIME ★

2 ounces (60 ml) gin

5 ounces (150 ml) Snapple lemon iced tea
(or other sweet tea brand)

6 drops absinthe

Ice

2 lemon slices

This is a truly twisted version of a Southern classic—sweet tea. We always make sure we have no plans to operate heavy machinery after drinking these herbalicious beverages.

Place gin, tea, and absinthe in a pint glass. Fill with ice, cover, and shake thoroughly. Garnish with lemon slices.

YIELD: 1 drink

★ BLUE LIPS ★

1½ ounces (42 ml) vodka (the cheaper the better)

½ ounce (14 ml) orange juice

Juice and peel from ½ lemon

½ ounce (14 ml) simple syrup (page 209)

3 ounces (90 ml) Gatorade Blue

Ice

This is a perfect example of how we make do with the gas station convenience store—and you can, too. It won't matter how cold it is when you have this drink at your tailgate, or when you're standing in a field over your barbecue rig. It will warm you from the inside out, so any tinge on your lips will come from the cocktail, not your body temperature.

Pour vodka, orange and lemon juices, syrup, and Gatorade into a pint glass, add ice, cover, and shake vigorously. Strain into whatever small cup you can get, and garnish with lemon peel.

YIELD: 1 drink

★ THE MEXICAN ★

Canned whipped cream

1 ounce (28 ml) sweetened condensed milk

½ ounce (14 ml) simple syrup (page 209)

2 dashes Tabasco sauce

1 ounce (28 ml) tequila reposado

4 ounces (120 ml) hot coffee

Hot sauce helps cut through the richness of the whipped cream and condensed milk in this riff on a traditional Mexican coffee. It's usually served after dinner, but it ain't bad for breakfast. As our friend Uncle Jed says, "You can't drink all day without starting early in the morning."

Prepare whipped cream by carefully purging the gas from the top of can so that it does not go in your mouth!

Combine condensed milk, simple syrup, and Tabasco sauce in a coffee mug, stirring with a spoon. Stir in tequila. Add hot coffee and garnish with whipped cream.

YIELD: 1 drink

RESOURCES

INSTRUCTIONAL

The BBQ Brethren: From the Backyard to the American Royal—www.bbq-brethren.com

The Virtual Weber Bullet—http://virtualweberbullet.com

ORGANIZATIONS

Caribbean BBQ Association—www.bbqpr.com

Florida Bar-B-Que Association—http://flbbq.org

German Barbecue Association—www.gbaev.de

Illinois BBQ Society—http://ilbbqs.com

New England BBQ Society—http://nebs.org

Iowa Barbeque Society—http://iabbq.org

Kansas City Barbeque Society—www.kcbs.us

Lonestar Barbecue Society—www.lonestarbarbecue.com

Memphis Barbecue Association (Memphis in May)— www.memphisinmay.org

Memphis Barbecue Network—www.mbnbbq.com

Mid-Atlantic Barbecue Association—www.mabbqa.com

North Carolina Barbecue Society—www.ncbbqsociety.com

Pacific Northwest BBQ Association—http://pnwba.com

Swiss Barbecue Association—http://worldteam.ch/5/Home.html

OUR FAVORITE GLOVES

Raw food: Black nitrile exam gloves— www.unisafedirect.com

Heat protection: Neoprene-coated insulated gloves— www.coleparmer.com, www.amazon.com

THERMOMETERS

Super-fast Thermapen—www.thermoworks.com

Probe thermometer—www.polder.com/dith.html, www.amazon.com

DRAFT CONTROL SYSTEMS

The BBQ Guru—http://thebbqguru.com

SMOKERS WE LIKE

Backwoods Smoker—http://backwoods-smoker.com

Big Green Egg—www.biggreenegg.com

Jambo Pits—www.jambopits.com

Spicewine Ironworks—http://spicewineironworks.com

Stump's Smokers—www.stumpssmokersinc.com

Weber Smokey Mountain—http://weber.com/explore/grills/smokers-series

AMERICAN WAGYU AND KUROBUTA PORK

Snake River Farms—http://snakeriverfarms.com

HARD-TO-FIND INGREDIENTS

Competition injection marinades—www.butcherbbq.com

Activa RM Transglutaminase (meat glue) and soy lecithin—http://willpowder.net, www.amazon.com

Spices, chile peppers, and chili powder blends— www.thespicehouse.com, http://penderys.com, www.amazon.com

Hickory powder—www.spicebarn.com/hickory_smoke_powder.htm

Long peppers—www.salttraders.com/products/Long-Pepper.html

Szechuan peppers—www.thespicehouse.com/spices/sichuan-peppercorns

Prague Powder #1 (pink salt)—www.sausagesource.com/catalog/ssm-acj-8oz.html

Blues Hog products—http://blueshog.com

ABOUT THE AUTHORS

Andy Husbands, the award-winning chef/owner of Tremont 647, has been enticing patrons with his adventurous American cuisine at the South End neighborhood restaurant and bar for well more than a decade. A James Beard "Best Chef" semi-finalist, Husbands competed in the sixth season of Fox Television Network's *Hell's Kitchen* with Gordon Ramsay. When he's not in the kitchen or working with his favorite charities, Husbands is on the BBQ trail with his award-winning team, iQUE. His first cookbook, *The Fearless Chef,* is currently in its second printing.

Chris Hart, winner of the Jack Daniel's Invitational World Championship in 2009, has dominated the competition BBQ circuit for the past 10 years with his team, iQUE. The team were the first northerners in barbecue history to win a World Championship. Hart spends his days developing software, but his passion for cooking barbecue has him following the competition BBQ trail on weekends, pitting his talents against the best pitmasters in the U.S. In 2010, Hart cooked an elaborate barbecue tasting menu at the James Beard House in NYC. In 2011, he competed in the Food Network's inaugural season of *Best in Smoke.*

Andrea Pyenson has been writing about food for more than a decade and enjoying it for a lot longer than that. Her writing about food and travel has appeared in *The Boston Globe, edible Boston, edible Cape Cod,* msn.com, oneforthetable.com, *The Washington Post,* and *Fine Cooking,* among others. Pyenson was associate editor of *The Boston Globe Illustrated New England Seafood Cookbook* and assistant editor of *52 Weeks Cheap Eats: Dining Deals in Greater Boston.*

ACKNOWLEDGMENTS

ANDY WOULD LIKE TO THANK . . .

My family, especially Miss Tessa, the cutest niece ever, for their love and support.

My brothers in the IQUE barbecue team: Kenny Goodman, Ed Doyle, Jamie Hart, Chris Hart, Dave Frary, and John Delpha for all the years of barbecue, poker, and bourbon; these are some of the best times ever.

Our IQUE team sponsor, Harpoon Brewery. Realfood Consultants for their outside-the-box thinking.

The hardworking and dedicated staff of Tremont 647 and Sister Sorel, especially Bonnie Nag.

Erin Bevan, for recipe development.

Jeff Elliot, for keeping me supplied with Henckels knives.

Joe Yonan, for recipe contribution from *The Fearless Chef*.

Ken Goodman, of Ken Goodman Photography, for his wonderful photographs and (sometimes) wise words.

Chris Hart, for his tenacious barbecue skills, creativity, writing, and friendship. And Andrea Pyenson for her wonderful writing and editing skills. It was an intense project, and I am honored to work with both of you.

CHRIS WOULD LIKE TO THANK . . .

My family—Jenny, Ethan, and Jaimie—for teaching me that food is love.

My brother and best friend, Jamie, and my niece, Sydney.

Mom, for inspiring me to cook.

Dad, for the unwavering support.

National BBQ champion Rod Gray and "the Godfather" Johnny Trigg for teaching me some of the finer points of championship barbecue.

Also, Andrea and Andy, thank you for this amazing experience.

ANDREA WOULD LIKE TO THANK . . .

My mother, for inspiring what I do in the kitchen; my father, for inspiring what I do on the page; and my sister, for always understanding.

My support group, Lisa Zwirn, Cathy Walthers, Rachel Travers, and Clara Silverstein, for all the advice and positive reinforcement.

Ken Goodman, for bringing this book alive with your spectacular photos. And Jenny Hart, for letting us invade your home for photo shoots.

Chris Hart, "the T.K. of BBQ." And Andy. At times this project felt overwhelming, but you always brought it back to fun. I've learned so much from both of you.

My boys. Craig and Luke, who make me laugh, make me so proud, and keep me focused on what's really important. And Eric, I can't ever thank you enough for your limitless patience, hand holding (literal and figurative), humor, and support, not to mention your barbecue skills.

WE ALL WANT TO THANK . . .

Our incredible recipe testers, with a special nod to Nancy Boyce and Kirsten Mikalson, who take their calling to another plane. Rachel Alabiso, Sarah Blackburn, Mike Boisvert, Brendan Burek, Adam Danforth, John Delpha, Sorel Denholtz, Diva Q Danielle Bennet Domovski, Alison Hardy, Karen Horton, Harriet Husbands, Ernie Kim, Bryan Simmons, Brys Stephens, and Mike "baaaaaahbecuuuuue" Sullivan all did an amazing job, with often challenging recipes and time constraints, as did ingredient hunter Amanda Poekert.

John Delpha and Jackson Cannon, for recipe development.

Dalyn Miller, for introducing us to Quayside Publishing. Agent extraordinaire Lisa Ekus and her team at The Lisa Ekus Group. Will Kiester and Jill Alexander of Quayside for concept development, editorial support, and challenging us with this project.

INDEX